# What to Say to Get What You Want

## OTHER BOOKS BY THE AUTHORS

by Sam Deep and Lyle Sussman

*Smart Moves: 14 Steps to Keep Any Boss Happy,
8 Ways to Start Meetings On Time, and
1600 More Tips to Get the Best from Yourself
and the People Around You*

*COMEX: The Communication Experience in
Human Relations*

by Sam Deep

*Human Relations in Management*

*A Program of Exercises for Management and
Organizational Behavior,* with James A. Vaughan

*Introduction to Business: A Systems Approach,*
with William D. Brinkloe

*Studies in Organizational Psychology,*
with Bernard M. Bass

*Current Perspectives for Managing Organizations,*
with Bernard M. Bass

by Lyle Sussman

*Communication for Supervisors and Managers*

*Increasing Supervisory Effectiveness*

# What to Say to Get What You Want

**Strong Words for 44 Challenging Types of Bosses, Employees, Coworkers, and Customers**

## Sam Deep & Lyle Sussman

**ADDISON-WESLEY PUBLISHING COMPANY**
Reading, Massachusetts    Menlo Park, California    New York
Don Mills, Ontario    Wokingham, England    Amsterdam    Bonn
Sydney    Singapore    Tokyo    Madrid    San Juan
Paris    Seoul    Milan    Mexico City    Taipei

Library of Congress Cataloging-in-Publication Data

Deep, Samuel D.
　　What to say to get what you want : strong words for 44 challenging
types of bosses, employees, coworkers, and customers / Sam Deep and
Lyle Sussman.
　　　　p.　　cm.
　　Includes index.
　　ISBN 0-201-57712-7
　　1. Vocational guidance.　2. Interpersonal communication.
I. Sussman, Lyle, 1944-　　II. Title.
HF5381.D423　1992
650.1—dc20　　　　　　　　　　　　　　　　　　　　91-19465
　　　　　　　　　　　　　　　　　　　　　　　　　　　　CIP

Cover design by Marge Anderson
Text design by Karen Savary
Set in 11-point Aster by Shepard Poorman Communications Corporation

6 7 8 9 10–MW–96959493
Sixth printing, August 1993

Addison-Wesley books are available at special discounts for bulk
purchases by corporations, institutions, and other organizations. For
more information, please contact:

Special Markets Department
Addison-Wesley Publishing Company
Reading, MA 01867
(617) 944-3700 x 2431

*To Di, David, Joe, Amy, and Melanie*
　　　　　　　　　*—S.D.*

*To Susie, Sandy, and Annie*
　　　　　　　　　*—L.S.*

*for helping us to remember the importance of listening*

# Contents

# Contents

# Introduction

**The people in our seminars** forced us to write this book.

Not that those people are uncooperative. In fact, managers who seek training are usually very open to change and to working with others. Rather, audience members often take us aside during breaks to say, "What do you do about a boss who never listens?" Or, "How can I get my assistant to be more positive?" Or, "I work with someone who takes credit for everyone else's ideas." Or, "You just wouldn't believe what a customer did in my store last week. . . . "

Those are difficult requests to fulfill when we're dying for a drink of water, wondering if we have time to dash into the men's room, or worrying that we have too much material for the rest of the day. Indeed, those are challenging questions at any time!

We once thought that our seminars answered all the questions thrown at us, and that these podium ambushers just hadn't been listening or were too impatient to wait for what was coming after the break. But we came to our senses during one of our too infrequent meetings in the USAir Club at the Pittsburgh Airport. We *were* giving people what they needed to cope with the challenging people in their lives, but we weren't giving it to them in the right form. Those managers were telling us, "I lead horses to water, but I can't get them to drink."

People need to learn specific techniques to move others toward the behavior they want. They also need to learn how to meet the challenge of nasty, troubled, demanding, aggressive, or unthinking people. We decided to reveal these techniques in a book—this book.

Our first strategy is to provide readers with the principles undergirding the techniques. We have termed these rules "The Ten Commandments of Change." Each chapter in the first half of the book describes one of the commandments.

We chose the term "commandment" with full recognition of its connotations. First, a commandment is an inviolable guiding principle. Break it and you risk the very happiness and success you're seeking. Second, the validity of a commandment cuts across contexts—it holds true regardless of the situation. This is not an "it all depends" book. The principles found here tell you how to deal with people regardless of who, what, when, and where. Finally, like other commandments, ours are derived from a solid foundation of workable truths. The ten you are about to read stem from:

- More than fifty years of collective experience as teachers, trainers, and consultants.
- The thousands of articles, studies, and books we've digested—the thoughts of untold philosophers, theologians, social scientists, and managers.

■ Observations of hundreds of cases where horses were led to water, with notations of when they drank and when they didn't.

The commandment chapters each begin with a vignette bearing remarkable similarity to a real situation we've observed where the subject commandment was breached. Then, with occasional help from that vignette, the chapter presents all the reasons why that commandment is typically violated, and tells you what to say and do to get the most out of difficult people.

More "what to say . . . " advice is found in the second half of the book: our advisories. For years we've kept notes on the difficult people described to us by thousands of frustrated managers and employees. We've assembled profiles of forty-four of the most aggressive, obnoxious, and frustrating people you are likely to encounter at work, together with hints on how to deal with them.

Now you can prepare yourself for your next confrontation with any of these forty-four characters. First, read the typical automatic responses to avoid—they will either get you into trouble or perpetuate the very behavior you seek to change. Armed with that warning, study the specific recommendations of what you should do and say in each situation. We give you sample scripts of conversations you might have with such people. Use these scripts as guidelines for your next encounter, or create your own based on ours.

We believe that if you study the Ten Commandments of Change and the advisories, you'll learn how to get the horse to drink. The secret is simple—make the horse thirsty. A thirsty horse will always drink!

# What to Say to Get What You Want

# I

# The Ten
Commandments
of Change

# 1

## Expect the Best

*Never negotiate excellence. You deserve to be the best you can be. If others prevent you from achieving your best, you must help them realize that both of you suffer by settling for mediocrity. You never achieve your potential by accepting "Good enough," "What's the use of trying?" "It's not gonna make any difference anyway," or, "What else can you expect from those kind of people?" You will never get what you want to get if you accept your current state as the best you'll ever get, or if you allow others to give you less than they are capable of giving.*

## The Burnout

Milt is in his late forties and is tired. "No doubt about it," he says, "I'm the guy they're writing about in all those career management books." After a fairly rapid rise up the ladder in his company, he finds himself in a job without any personal challenge and without prospects for further advancement.

In a coaching and counseling session with one of us Milt laid it all out: "If I had to do it over again, I don't know if I'd sell my body and soul to corporate America. I gave them the most productive years of my life, and it looks like I'm gonna get kicked in the teeth for it. For all I know, I'll be here about as long as it takes them to fill my job with someone who's half my age and will work for half the pay.

"At this point I'm just going through the motions. I'm doing the minimum to keep my job. Why try to do more when it's not rewarded by the top guns? And I'm not the only one around here who feels that way. Most of my peers started in this company at a time when we could bank on job security and advancement if we put in a hard day's work. We also had people reporting to us who put in long hard hours and who cared about the quality of their work. Boy, are those days gone forever!

"I know I'm not being totally honest with this company by easing up, but the way I feel, I don't give a damn. And for the life of me I don't know what to do about it. Even if there was something to do, I don't know if I would. I mean, what's the use?"

A long time ago, Milt gave up. He no longer expects the best out of himself or out of his company. He and his family will suffer because of it, and his company is losing his capability to contribute. Why?

## Why We Violate This Commandment

You may now be thinking, "Expect the best? Tell us something we don't know." But it's one thing to know something is common sense; it's quite another for your actions to support that belief. Just as we espouse the golden rule while acting otherwise, many ambitious people behave as if they do *not* expect the best. There are at least four reasons why this first commandment is violated.

### We Believe that We Don't Deserve Any Better

Each of us knows a Milt. We might be working next to him, under him, or over him. We might live with a Milt. And some of us might find him in the mirror.

Some people just don't expect excellence because

they believe they don't deserve it or they can't attain it. Once a Milt "accepts his fate," a self-fulfilling prophecy kicks in. Because he doesn't expect the best, he doesn't try for the best, and less than the best is exactly what he gets—not because of misfortune but because he denied it to himself.

## We've Become Cynical

Unfortunately, each of us has been in a relationship (working or otherwise) where the other person was dishonest, apathetic, or willing to settle for good enough. However, just because we find ourselves working with these people does not necessarily mean that all people are dishonest, apathetic, and marginal, or that we are obliged to settle for second best.

Look around you for the signs of masterful accomplishment. Every day, scientists are announcing treatments for diseases that were once thought to be untreatable. Companies that started out in garages or kitchens (Apple Computer, Hewlett-Packard) have joined the ranks of the *Fortune* 500. Individuals born with the handicaps of poverty or physical disability have become leaders of society. Yes, there are plenty of incompetents and ne'er-do-wells, but there are countless others in our society who strive for the best.

If you believe that people who strive for quality and set high standards for themselves are the exception rather than the rule, then you are destined to perpetuate your frustration. Someone once defined a cynic as a person who smells roses and looks around for a casket. Cynicism is self-defeating. If you expect people to give you mediocrity, you will get mediocrity. If you expect the best because you honestly believe people can give you the best, you'll be amazed at how often they deliver. The German philosopher Goethe said, "Treat people as if they were what they ought to be, and you help them become what they are capable of being."

## We Settle for Second Best Because It's Easy

One view of humans is as "economic maximizers," constantly seeking to increase personal benefits while reducing personal costs and risks. This behavior leads us down the path of least resistance. Second best *is* often the path of least resistance. We cut our personal risk by accepting "good enough" rather than pushing for what we know is better.

For many people the concept of "cost" relates to money. Yet there are other kinds of costs you can incur when you strive for the best. There's the possibility that you might not achieve the goals you've set, and have to live with what you see as failure. Or your accomplishment may go unrecognized, resulting in frustration. And consider the costs of pushing other people to produce their best:

- the anxiety of having to confront a colleague who is causing you grief and frustration.
- the discomfort of telling subordinates that their performance is not up to standard.
- the frustration associated with coaching and counseling those who want to achieve but don't have the skills or resources.

Indeed, the high personal cost of improving poor performance makes it easier to overlook it—easier, but not better. Those who settle for the easy way out trade short gain for long-term loss. Kids who are picked up after learn that it's okay to play without cleaning up. This lesson hurts both the children and the parents. Employees who are never given challenging assignments are taught that they can't be trusted and their skills are minimal. This lesson hurts both the boss and the employee. You won't get the best from yourself or others if you aren't willing to pay the price. View the initial cost as an investment that will pay off in the long run. Is it tough to expect and work for the best? Absolutely! Is it worth it? You bet it is!

## Our Biases Condition Us to Set Low Standards

We return to Milt. His output depends largely on the performance of two employees, Frank and Sheila. Frank has worked at the company for many years. He once told Milt about growing up in a Midwestern town that could have been the birthplace of Andy Hardy. In school, in church, and at his prestigious college Frank saw people like himself—white, Anglo-Saxon, Protestant. Throughout his formative years, he was told to be leery of blacks, Jews, Asians, and Hispanics. Milt knows that Frank doesn't trust such people to perform on his level or with his commitment.

Sheila, on the other hand, is a young black woman. She was recruited right out of community college, at a job fair which the company cosponsored as part of its affirmative action program. She is the first person in her family with a white-collar job. Even after a year at the company, Sheila comes to Milt at least once a day for help. She doesn't ask Frank for advice because he grumbles about how some people can't handle simple tasks. Milt knows Sheila is trying her best, so he avoids criticizing her. Rather than showing her what she has done wrong, Milt ends up doing her work for her.

The primary problem in this department isn't Sheila's inexperience or Frank's overt prejudice, nasty and painful as that is. Instead, Milt's hidden prejudices are even more harmful. People with hidden prejudices appear open and direct ("This is what I expect you to do") but have a contradictory hidden agenda ("I really don't expect you to change or to become a major contributor to this team"). When we have covert prejudices, we set low expectations for other people.

Milt doesn't push Sheila to master new tasks because he doesn't want to "punish" her for not having received a privileged education. Nor does he expect Frank to work well with Sheila because he couldn't help being taught that minorities and women are inferior. In both cases Milt has told himself that his employees can't do any better than they're doing. As a result, Frank retains his prejudice, Sheila learns that her boss doesn't expect her to do her best, and Milt's output lags.

Milt needs to make it clear to Frank that the modern American company is more than Tom, Dick, and Harry—it is also Luong, Carlos, and Mary. And Milt needs to train Sheila to handle all her responsibilities, no matter how much extra initial effort that requires. Most of all, Milt needs to tell himself to expect the best.

## How to Implement This Commandment

Can we overcome violations of the First Commandment? Of course. What follows are simple and practical suggestions to help you "expect the best."

### Stop Living in the Past

The only thing you can and should do about what happened yesterday is to learn from it. Yesterday, good or bad, is history. Tomorrow is a dream, a hope, a passion. Don't let your history destroy your dream.

You have two choices in dealing with old disappointments. One is to be forever burdened by what you see as an unjust, impoverished, or unfulfilling past. The other is to live today as if you have a brand new chance to prove that you can succeed. *Carpe Diem!* Seize the Day! Think of the jet plane—it has no rear view mirror. As you speed to the future, you'll have no need for one either.

### Commit Yourself to Personal Development Goals

You may be experiencing burnout; you may be at a stage in your career when you are more concerned with simply staying on the path than in blazing new trails. Someone once said that if you're part of a team, you've got to do one of three things: lead, follow, or get out of the way. Decide what's best for you and for your team. If you no longer want to push for the best, that's a choice you have a right to make. But don't sabotage the efforts of others by making them pull you along. You owe it to everyone to get energized and pursue the "thrill of victory."

Set goals for yourself that will make you the best you can be. You don't get what you deserve; you get what you create. Create a tomorrow for yourself. If you don't fashion it, someone else will.

What personal development goals do you have? Is there a language you want to learn? A skill you need to acquire? A relationship you should improve? Without personal development goals you will either stagnate or develop merely by reacting to your environment.

The word "successes" has four s's in it—the same four s's that each of your personal development goals must pass through. Personal development goals that lead to successes are specific, seen, said, and scribbled. Let us show you what this means.

Consider the goal of "becoming a more effective supervisor." Immediately, it fails to pass through the first "s"—it's not *specific* and therefore unmeasurable. If your personal development goal is too broadly focused, first ask yourself, "Why do I have this goal?" You may have to answer this question more than once to get down to your specific underlying motivation. Once you understand, you're ready to state your goal succinctly. For example: "To sell my ideas more successfully to my subordinates."

The second "s"—*seen*—is a bit easier, but no less important. Imagine yourself as a successful motivator. You may have to close your eyes to see yourself in a specific situation with a particular person. How does it look? How does it sound? How does it feel? Now that you have "seen" your goal, are you still committed to it? Did you learn anything that will help you to attain it?

The third test for your personal development goal is to *say* it to yourself and to others. This helps to cement your commitment and gains potential support for your effort. When others hear of your plan, they may give you feedback on how they perceive its value, or advise you on how to attain it: "I attended a great seminar on motivation skills—here's the number to call for information."

Finally, a goal is nothing more than a wish until it is *scribbled* down. Your commitment is sealed when your goal flows through a pen onto a piece of paper— especially when you keep that piece of paper where you'll see it often. The benefit of this fourth "s" is enhanced when you go beyond a mere restatement of the goal. Magnify its power by also scribbling your *plan of achievement*—write down each of the *what's* ("Call the Management Development Seminar Company for their next offering in our city.") and the *when's* ("9:00 AM tomorrow").

## Don't Accept Excuses Without Solutions

When a subordinate comes to you with an excuse for why the project is late ("People quit," "It was more complex than we thought," "It's costing more than we anticipated"), refuse to listen to the excuse unless it is followed by a plan of action. Managers are paid to achieve results—not to analyze reasons for failure. Create an expectation within your work group that when things go wrong, you fix problems, not blame. This will encourage them to come to you with bold solutions, not defensive excuses.

When subordinates come to you for solutions, bite your tongue until you hear theirs. Don't let them think that they're paid to listen and do while you're paid to talk and think. When they dump problems in your lap, ask, "What have you done so far?" If they say, "Nothing," either send them back to think about your question or say, "What will you do *next* time before you bring something like this to my attention?" Before offering any final solutions, ask them for theirs. If they cannot think of one, say, "Well, if you *could* think of something, what would it be?" You'll be amazed how often this clever probe works.

## Set Goals that Force People to Expand

Never accept what you can achieve unless that achievement has forced you and your team to stretch. A goal should be challenging but not daunting. It should be motivating because it can be attained, not frustrating because it's impossible to attain.

In recent years we've been inundated with analyses of the Japanese turnaround following their devastating defeat in World War II. Although many reasons account for Japan's current status in international markets, one can be found in a single word: *Kaizen*. *Kaizen* means constant and upward improvement. The Japanese culture is based on the premise that processes must constantly be improved—that regardless how productive you are today, you can be even more productive tomorrow. Compare this philosophy with the standard American response to change and improvement: "If it ain't broke, don't fix it."

Force yourself and those under your influence to disavow the "ain't broke" mentality and to start thinking in terms of *Kaizen*. Emphasize that the process can always be improved. Reward their ideas for how to turn out a better product. Demonstrate your commitment to the highest possible levels of organizational quality.

### Provide Coaching to Help Others Achieve Their Goals

Bobby Knight, one of the top college basketball coaches in the country, describes success and failure this way: "The difference between winners and losers is not that winners have the will to win. Even losers have the will to win. The difference is that winners have the will to prepare."

You do no good by simply setting goals and telling people to "do your best." Help them attain their best. Remember: will + skill = success. Be available to them with your time, your advice, and your support. Get the finest training available for them. Empower them to succeed.

### Recognize that Your Biases Are Self-Destructive

Treating others as if they can't or won't achieve will ultimately hurt you. Your success depends on the people with whom you work. If you accept substandard performance as their best because of supposed "demographic limitations," you ultimately hurt yourself. You don't have to like everyone. You do have to expect the best from them. That is, if you want your team to survive and thrive.

## Exercise Your Rights in What to Expect from Others

Look at yourself in the mirror and tell the person you see: "You have rights. Some you are guaranteed by the Constitution. Some you deserve because you are a free-thinking, rational human being." Specifically:

- You have a right not to be victimized, physically or psychologically, by others.
- You have a right to refuse to solve other people's problems.
- You have a right to ask someone else to change his or her behavior if that behavior victimizes you or others.
- You have a right to dislike other people—but not to discriminate against them.
- You have a right to say no.
- You have a right to *expect the best*.

## The Essence of the First Commandment

- Stop Living in the Past
- Commit Yourself to Personal Development Goals

- Don't Accept Excuses Without Solutions
- Set Goals that Force People to Expand
- Provide Coaching to Help Others Achieve Their Goals
- Recognize that Your Biases Are Self-Destructive
- Exercise Your Rights In What to Expect from Others

---

*If you always do what you've always done,*
*you'll always get what you've always got.*

ANONYMOUS

# 2

# Listen Before Talking; Think Before Acting

*Your ear keeps your foot out of your mouth. Ask questions; listen to the answers. Find out what people want and why they want it. Think about the consequences of your actions before you speak and before you act. Put yourself in other people's shoes in order to anticipate their reactions. You can move people by understanding why they believe what they believe, and then adapting your message to accommodate that belief. You can't achieve this goal if you're not listening to them or if you're acting irrationally.*

## The Expert

Tony was promoted to the manager's job because he was one of the best salespeople the store ever had. The store policy had always favored promotion from within. Based on his past performance, it looked as if the policy was highly appropriate in Tony's case. He was smart, aggressive, well liked by his coworkers, and had a talent for satisfying customers' needs.

Two weeks into the job, however, it became obvious that Tony was uncomfortable with the mantle of "store manager," and this discomfort was affecting relationships with his staff and customers.

Mark Edwards, district manager and unofficial troubleshooter for the company, was sent to find out what was happening in the store, and to coach Tony if necessary. Within minutes of arriving at the store, Mr. Edwards set up personal interviews with each employee. He wanted to hear in their own words what they thought the problem was.

At the end of the day of interviews his notebook revealed the following employee observations:

- "Tony refuses to listen to any of us. He makes

decisions unilaterally even if we know more about the situation than he does."

- "He often interrupts during meetings. We never get a chance to finish our thoughts or tell him what we're thinking. In those rare instances when he does ask us our opinion, you know he's not really interested in our answer. He's only appeasing us."

- "This job's getting to him. He flies off the handle too easily. Yesterday he yelled at a salesclerk in front of other employees. He was never this insensitive when he was a salesman like us. I recently saw him talk back to a customer who was complaining about shoes she bought that morning. Tony almost got into a shouting match with her."

Tony, himself, had the last interview of the day. Mr. Edwards began with an open-ended question: "Tony, what do you think might account for the store's poor performance?"

Tony stared at the ground for a few seconds and in a hushed, hesitant voice said:

"I'm responsible. I felt pressured the moment you guys promoted me. I thought that I had to show everyone in the store who was boss. I didn't want them to step all over me or take advantage of me because I used to work with them and partied with them. I also wanted to show you guys in headquarters that you made the right decision by promoting me. That's why I followed my own course rather than listening to the guys in the store. After all, why promote me if you don't want me to make the decisions? But the pressure was getting so bad that I guess I was losing my cool and flying off the handle. Mr. Edwards, please, I need your help. What do you think I should do?"

## Why We Violate This Commandment

We'd all like to think that we are rational beings, capable of self-control, and manifesting mature "give and take" in our relations with others. Yet if there were an unobtrusive video camera randomly recording our conversations, we might be shocked by the drastic difference between what we think we do and what we actually do. Many of us would find that, contrary to the image we'd like to project—an image of self-control and empathy—we actually think and act impulsively. We talk without listening and act without thinking. And when we do, we invariably fail to influence other people.

There are at least four major reasons why we violate this second commandment.

### We Believe that We Waste Time Listening to Counterarguments

Someone once said that there are two sides to every argument—until you take one of them. As soon as you decide that one position represents the side of truth, reason, and justice, it follows that the opposing side must be false and unjust. Moreover, once we take a given position we also close our minds to any information which might challenge our view.

Tony wasn't listening to his employees because he labored under the erroneous belief that the boss had to be right. He thought he would be seen as weak if he asked questions or sought help from his employees. He also believed that he was promoted because upper management trusted his talent and judgment. He was simply doing what he thought he should do—applying the judgment and instincts that got him the promotion in the first place.

## We Give In to Anger and Frustration

The boiling point for water is 100°C at sea level. This is a law of nature. Unfortunately, the "boiling point" for people cannot be expressed so precisely. Human boiling points are as variable as the people who populate our planet. Some people will go berserk at the least provocation; others seem to have the patience of Job.

Nevertheless, we can state a law of human behavior and emotion: unlike other species, we can control our emotions. No one but you can make you angry. You can respond rationally even under the most irrational circumstances. You can choose to control your emotions, or your emotions can control you. It's your decision.

Tony was feeling pressured and frustrated in his new job. He reached his boiling point, yelled at employees, and became confrontational with customers. He could and should have controlled his emotions. Unfortunately, he did not and suffered the consequences.

When you fail to control your emotions, you stop thinking with your head and start thinking with your tongue or your fists. You do or say things you later regret. And the tragic irony is that in your attempt to persuade another, you create just the opposite effect. A potential ally has turned into a volcano of retribution. The other person not only rejects your position, but looks for ways to sabotage your efforts.

You do have a right to feel angry, frustrated, or any other emotion. Tony had a right to feel what he was feeling. However, neither you nor Tony should allow this right to turn into a mandate to act without thinking.

## We Value What We Have to Say More Than What We Have to Hear

For years we have conducted seminars on effective communication. When participants review the agenda, they often wonder: "Why spend so much time on *listening* skills?" The unstated premise of the question gets to the heart of why we violate the Second Commandment. Most of us believe that we communicate assertively when we send out messages, not when we take them in. Therefore, a course on effective communication should focus on how you should get your message to the other person, not vice versa. Our approach to communication, however, forces our seminar participants to question that premise.

We say you're a good communicator because you're a good listener. You get your message across because first you allow the other person's message to get in. You know what to say because you have listened well enough to know what will influence the other person. You also make the other person feel better about you and your subsequent messages.

Another reason most of us believe that what we have to say is more important than what we have to hear is due to our method of influencing others. When trying to get a person to do something, most of us fall into habitual thought patterns that lead to self-defeating questions:

- What can I say to get the person to do this?

- What's the most persuasive argument I can use?

- What's the best way of phrasing the request?

- Should I test my pitch on someone else?

- Will threats help?

These questions are all based on what you have to say—a self-centered approach that's therefore doomed to fail.

Compare the previous set of questions with these:

- Why is the person resisting my request?

- What's happening in the person's life right now that causes this resistance?

- What are the person's ambitions, goals, fears, and passions?

- What will my idea do for the person?

- What counterarguments are likely to be used against my request?

This set of questions is based on what the person has to hear in order to be convinced. These questions imply the use of a listener-centered strategy—a strategy with excellent chances for success.

Tony never asked himself any of these questions. If he had, his problems would not have occurred.

## We're More Concerned with Our Needs Than the Needs of Others

You may have seen the bags from Stew Leonard's stores that state:

- Rule 1: The customer is always right!
- Rule 2: If the customer is ever wrong, reread Rule 1.

This simple law says that in order to serve customers better, all transactions must be viewed through the customer's eyes—regardless of how jaundiced, myopic, or blind they might be.

You start to change others the moment you look at the problem through their eyes and hear the problem through their ears. Tony was so concerned with meeting his boss's expectations that he failed to look at the store through his employees' or his customers' eyes. His only concern was the frustration he was facing; he was oblivious to everything else. Again we see the tragic irony: the more he focused on his personal problems, the more problems he created for others, thereby creating more problems for himself.

## How to Implement This Commandment

The Second Commandment becomes part of your repertoire when you see the value of listening, practice active listening, learn to control your emotions, and anticipate the consequences of your actions.

### Change Your Attitude Toward Listening

Listening is not so much a skill as it is an attitude; therefore, the real trick in becoming a better listener is to want to be one. What is the incentive? Consider just a few of the advantages of listening over speaking:

- You give others the opportunity to vent.
- You gain knowledge about the right thing to say in response.
- You get ideas from others that will help you solve your problems.
- You earn the respect of the people you are trying to move.
- You avoid trouble—the outcome frequently achieved by mouths, rarely by ears.

Starting today, think of listening as essential to your personal and professional success; see it as a proactive, not a passive act. You begin to move others the moment you give them a good listening-to.

## Practice Active Listening

Follow these steps as you increase your commitment to listening:

- Focus on the other person. Engage in eye contact. Observe facial expressions. Sit or stand in an attentive position. Show that you are listening.

- Block out competing thoughts. Fight the temptation to engage in mental counterarguments. Your mind works four times faster than the average speaking rate: fight the temptation to wander off.

- Ask questions. Seek clarification. Probe for further meaning or hidden meaning. Listen for the unstated, implied message, not just the explicit stated message.

- Tell the other person what you think you heard. Negotiate any misunderstanding or misinterpretation ("Is this what you mean? Have I understood you correctly? Are you saying that . . . ?")

- Finally, respond to what you heard. Describe your agreement, surprise, and any other reaction to what was said.

## Control Your Anger and Frustration

People don't get you angry; you get angry. You may not be able to control what people do to you, but you can control how you respond.

When you feel yourself losing control, take a deep breath; inhale slowly and exhale slowly. And remember this when you get angry with others:

- An angry response is not likely to persuade, but *is* likely to make the other person angry. This is why a heated exchange changes few minds for the better.

- If the other person remains calm while you get angry, that person's presence of mind is likely to defeat you.

- Believe it or not, the person who is attracting your anger feels justified, just as you feel when you make others angry. Try to understand the reason for the person's behavior. Become analytical and you won't get angry.

- Talk about your anger. Directing yourself to your feelings will help you to calm down, and it will allow the conversation to move gradually to a more rational tone.

- Call a break for a cooling-off period whenever emotions flare. The moment you feel you're about to lose control, your rational brain is talking; listen to it. It's telling you that you're on the verge of doing or saying something you'll later regret. Remember, three things cannot be recalled: time passed, the spent arrow, and the spoken word.

- Finally, get out of the reach of incorrigible people and those who delight in getting to you. Work through intermediaries or buffers, if possible. When all else fails, separate from them; give them the rejection they've earned. (See the Tenth Commandment.)

## Anticipate the Consequences of Your Actions

Every action you take today will have an effect tomorrow. Before you try to change someone's behavior, consider the consequences if you succeed. For example, if you are about to convince a subordinate to take on increased responsibility, are you prepared to pay the price? Consider that you may have to:

1. Give the employee a larger raise at the next pay review period.
2. Take a great deal of time to explain the new responsibility, to train, to answer questions, and to evaluate performance.
3. Accept reduced performance in this responsibility until the employee becomes proficient at it.
4. Accept reduced performance in other areas, or take other responsibilities away from the employee.
5. Deal with other employees who may be angry because you did not give the responsibility to them.
6. Let the employee take over some of the most enjoyable parts of your job.

As you receive commitments from others to make new tomorrows, remember that those tomorrows are the reason for your efforts. Project yourself into the future. Think about all the possible ramifications of your request. Don't be so short-sighted that the tomorrow you create causes more pain than the today you want to escape.

## The Essence of the Second Commandment

- Change your attitude toward listening.
- Practice active listening.
- Control your anger and frustration.
- Anticipate the consequences of your actions.

*To say the right thing at the right time, keep still most of the time.*

JOHN W. ROPER

# 3

---

## Get to the Point

---

*A common reason why we fail to move people is that we don't tell them where we want them to go. Don't hint or beat around the bush. Make certain you know what you want and why you want it. Get feedback from others on your motivation. Meet with the person, state the problem, listen to explanations, and ask for the change you want.*

## Top Seller

A management consultant was called in to provide private coaching for a senior, high-performing travel agent in a large office. Although Marie Morgan was the top seller in the office, her behavior frustrated the agency's manager. She often flew off the handle with peers, tour operators, and clients, and was impatient with the young employees she was asked to train. The same drive she consistently channeled into high performance too often took the form of tongue lashings, icy stares, and sarcasm.

The manager was doubly frustrated because other employees looked up to Marie and often turned to her for help. Indeed, the manager had for some time viewed her as a role model, hoping that her success in generating business would rub off on other agents. But her volatile behavior, combined with a certain amount of jealousy, made her far less than a good example.

The agency manager requested coaching sessions so that Marie might recognize the impact of her behavior on the rest of the staff. The consultant braced for a difficult encounter, with high potential for defensiveness and denial. But confrontation never materialized, thanks to a simple oversight on the part of the manager. This oversight became apparent when the consultant casually referred to the manager's desire for Marie to lead the office through example.

Marie's response was, "Who, me? I never knew the manager saw me that way. She's always saying how important she believes it is for her to treat each of us the same. And frankly, with my experience I've resented it. I'm flattered that she wants me to be a role model, and I'd be willing to do what I can to control my temper and give the rest of the staff someone they can count on. She's always criticized my outbursts, but I never felt she reacted as critically with others. Now I know why. But why didn't she *ask* me to be a role model?"

Indeed, why didn't the agency manager tell Marie why it was so important to change her behavior? What prevents us from getting to the point and being direct with the difficult people in our lives?

## Why We Violate This Commandment

At the root of much of the frustration we feel with others is their failure to fulfill our expectations. Expectations are likely to be unfulfilled whenever they are *unrealistic,* given the ability or motivation of the other person. Neither are expectations likely to be met when they are *inappropriate* to the setting or to the other person's self-concept. Similarly, the more *numerous* they are—the more behaviors we hold others accountable to—the less likely they will all be met. However, the major reason we don't get what we want from others is that *we never ask for it;* in other words, we don't state our expectations.

## We Are Afraid to State Our Expectations

Fear is the major reason we don't tell others exactly what behavior we expect of them. This fear takes one or more of the following forms.

We may fear that we will appear presumptuous if we state clearly and unequivocally what we want. But if you ask people for *their expectations of you* at the same time you state your expectations of them, you're not being the least bit aggressive. Rather, you're being equally assertive for all concerned. A supervisor who meets with subordinates to show them her ten most important expectations for their performance will not be viewed negatively if, at the same time, she asks her staff for a statement of what behavior they require from her to fulfill their expectations.

Fear of rejection may also discourage you from telling others your expectations. You're not the only manager in this world who won't tell people exactly what you expect of them for fear that they will defy those expectations. Related to this is the common worry that by laying our cards on the table we'll put too much pressure on the other person, and will cause that person to feel like a failure.

A final fear to acknowledge is one that far more people experience than are willing to admit: the desire to avoid public statements of our underlying values.

Once we go on record with our requirements, others know more about us and are in a better position to make accurate judgments about what it will take to meet our needs. Some people hesitate to make such clear revelations of their needs for fear of being vulnerable to the devious motives of others. With some people in our lives this fear makes good sense; too often, however, we use this excuse to hide our expectations from *everyone*, and suffer misguided performance from them as a result.

In "Top Seller," the primary reason the travel agency manager never asked Marie in so many words to be a role model with younger employees was that she couldn't offer financial compensation or a promotion in exchange for the request, and was certain it would be rejected.

## We Assume Others Know What We Want

A second reason we fail to state our expectations to others is that we assume they already know. The behavior we desire is so apparent to us that we wrongly believe it is equally apparent to them.

A school board that was disappointed with the performance of the district's superintendent called in an educational consultant for help. After examining the situation, the consultant made her report. She informed the board of her judgment that the superintendent didn't seem to be aware of the exact nature of their dissatisfaction. She offered to assist the board in constructing a list of specific performance expectations for the superintendent along with a description of exactly what he might do regarding each expectation to demonstrate that he was doing his job. She was about to explain the time limit the board should give him for compliance when they erupted. In the sharp words of the board president: "Are you kidding? This man is a professional! He has a Ph.D.! He was a superintendent before he came here! Do you mean to tell us that he doesn't know how to do his job?" In other words, one of the Ph.D. courses that superintendent should have taken was Mind Reading.

Each relationship, whether at work or at home, has its own unique set of expectations in both directions. One of the best ways to keep all parties happy is to get our expectations out on the table before the relationship is ever struck. The school board described above ultimately fired their superintendent and asked the same consultant back to hire a new one. The consultant agreed under one condition: each finalist in the search would be given a list of the specific expectations—beyond the standard position description—that the board had for a superintendent. There turned out to be *twenty-two* different expectations.

## We Don't Know What We Want

A third reason we don't get to the point is that we don't know what it is ourselves. We become frustrated when our needs aren't met, and we get so enmeshed in that feeling of frustration (in our stomach) that we can't think clearly about a way out (with our head). We want others to meet our expectations, but we don't stop to think about what those expectations really are.

The agency manager in "Top Seller" knew that she wanted a positive role model in the office. Other than controlling anger and other negative behaviors, however, she didn't have a clear mental picture of how such an employee behaves in *positive* terms. She hadn't defined how that employee would function in relation to her duties or the duties of her assistant manager. When asked how a "role model" behaves she responded, "Well, I don't know, exactly. I just know that I want the others to look up to her." Marie couldn't do much with such ambiguity.

## How to Implement This Commandment

Getting to the point requires four steps. First, picture clearly the new behavior you seek from the other person. Second, be certain you are honest with yourself about why you want the other person's behavior to change. Tell the person the problems resulting from the status quo, and finally, ask for the change you want in specific terms.

### Picture the Change You Want

What exactly do you want the other person to do? What does the behavior look like, sound like, smell like, taste like, and feel like? Focus on the positive, not the negative. Fixate on what you want rather than on what you don't want, so that when you talk with the person you'll concentrate on something positive instead of something negative. Invent the future; don't dredge up the past.

Had the agency manager done this, she might have concluded she wanted the agent to:

1. Remain calm when things are going wrong.
2. Be patient with slow learning employees and answer their questions—even "stupid" ones—in a spirit of helpfulness.
3. Be tactfully assertive with uncooperative tour operators.
4. Be solicitous with clients who change itineraries, who don't follow instructions, or who have unrealistic expectations.
5. Spend ten percent of her time coaching and counseling less experienced employees.

### Know Why You Want the Change

What will the desired behavior achieve for you, the other person, and the organization to which you belong? Are you asking for change for the benefit of others, such as the accomplishment of the organization's goals, or are your motives selfish, such as control of the person or minimization of your personal risk? If your true purpose is to enhance some common good, then you should proceed. On the other hand, when selfish motives are behind your request, they often yield unfortunate long-term results.

The travel agency manager might have decided, "In order of importance, my motives are: (1) I want to avoid complaints from subordinates, tour operators, and customers when Marie acts up; (2) I want to increase the productivity of the staff, which will happen if Marie becomes a stabilizing rather than a disruptive influence; and (3) when she functions as a positive role model, I won't have to supervise the staff as closely."

Also consider how determined you are to work patiently with the person to induce change. Your persistence must exceed the other person's resistance. And the more passion you have to achieve your goal, the sooner you'll bring it about.

## Get Feedback on Your Motivation, Goals, and Strategy

Before you meet with the person to express your request, consult confidentially with one or more acquaintances whose judgment you trust. Ask for their advice on the validity of your goal and the appropriateness of your motivation. Consider their feedback before you proceed.

An independent assessment can help you distinguish your wants from your needs. For example, a small store owner consulted one of the authors on how to get his employees to accept the idea of wearing uniform smocks. The consultant's response was, "Why do you want them to wear smocks? What goal of yours will this achieve?"

The answer was, "So they'll look uniform."

The consultant's retort: "Why do you want them to look uniform?"

After several more answers and several more probes, the manager came to the realization that he really wanted his employees to improve customer service. This valid *need* bore little relationship to wearing smocks—a *want* that was discarded as soon as its irrelevance became apparent.

### State the Problem

Once you have a clear picture of your goal and your intent, you are ready to state the nature of the problem to the person. Follow these three steps:

1.  Describe the current situation. Tell the person what event, behavior, or performance concerns you. Give examples. Don't allow the first word out of your mouth to be "you." Focus on *what is happening* rather than on *what the person is doing* if that separation can be made.

2.  Tell the person exactly why and how the behavior creates a problem for the organization, for you, or for your relationship. Be specific.

3.  Tell the person how you feel about the situation. But don't be punitive or attempt to make the person feel guilty.

The travel agency manager could have stated this as the problem:

"The office climate isn't quite what we need in order to get top performance from our staff. What I consider to be one of the most influential components that could alter that climate is you. The other agents in this office look up to you—and so do I. Your sales last year were forty percent higher than anyone else's. While the others may never match you, they can do better with your help. Unfortunately, right now they hesitate to take advantage of your knowledge. The outbursts that you and I have discussed, and which are beginning to show improvement, still have them scared of you. For example, yesterday when you grew impatient with Helen's inability to grasp the new airline booking system, your statement that, 'You've been here three months and haven't learned a thing,' had her in tears in the bathroom for over half an hour. And similar situations have occurred with that tour operator who called you on Tuesday and that client who wrote the letter of complaint to headquarters last month.

"All this has me worried about three things. First, about my staff, who aren't getting what they need from my most valuable human asset in order for them to excel. Second, about the loyalty of our customers. And, finally, I care about you and your growth in this company. I want to see you receive performance reviews that match your sales figures, and that will position you for future advancement."

## Listen to Explanations

We are often certain that we know what's causing a problem behavior in others. You may have a good idea of their reasons for behaving the way they do, but you may be off base. Even if you don't really care what their reasons are, you do well to give them an opportunity to explain. In listening to their response to your statement of what's happening, why it's a problem, and how you feel about it, you may learn something that completely changes your view of the situation. And even if nothing new is added, you'll attain more cooperation by letting them vent whatever feelings they have built up.

## Ask for the Change You Want

Say what you want! Describe it in terms of a need you would like to have fulfilled. Be specific. Paint the clearest of pictures. Tell the person what the behavior will look like when it occurs. Don't hint or beat around the bush. Leave nothing to the person's imagination.

Take great care not to be punishing. Directness does not mean rudeness or thoughtlessness. Indeed, be as supportive, positive, and affirming as you can. Your optimism says that you care and encourages the effort to live up to your expectations.

The agency manager might ask for what she wants like this: "I need you to be a role model in this office. I would like employees to feel free to turn to you for the help that only you can give them. I want them to observe you treating customers courteously, cheerfully, and with model patience. I want your control, tact, and ongoing competence to set the standard for professionalism in this office. I want them to learn from you. Finally, I want to be able to give you at least ninety-five points out of one hundred on your next quarterly performance review."

## The Essence of the Third Commandment

- Picture the change you want.
- Know why you want the change.
- Get feedback on your motivation, your goals, and your strategy.
- State the problem to the person.
- Listen to explanations.
- Ask for the change you want.

*Tact is the art of making a point without making an enemy.*

HOWARD W. NEWTON

# 4

# Change What They Do, Not Who They Are

*Attitudes may cause behavior, but they are difficult, if not impossible, to change. However, almost any new behavior that is repeated twenty-one times becomes a habit. And that habit eventually begins to generate a new attitude that reinforces the behavior.*

## The Sexist

Jack Sterns "paid his dues" for thirty-three years before being named Vice President for Manufacturing at Intertech, a large engineering company. His career began on the shop floor. A great deal of hard work and a slow but steady stream of promotions finally landed him in the corporate board room.

The Chief Operating Officer's decision to promote Jack over several younger candidates was proving to be a good one. He brought a wealth of experience, which he immediately put to work correcting production shortcomings. At the same time, he was spearheading several initiatives that promised to improve quality control far beyond what had been achieved under his predecessors. Jack's years of experience were paying off for Intertech.

Unfortunately, one dark cloud loomed over Jack's first year in office. As reported by the Vice President for Human Resources to the C.O.O., three female supervisors, two female manufacturing managers, and the Vice President for Communications had all complained within the past ten days about Jack. They each accused him of sexist behavior.

First, there was Jack's language. He habitually

---

referred to women as "girls," "sweet young ladies," or "honey." And his language reflected his deep-seated attitude; he valued male input more than that of women. This favoritism was blatant in Jack's reactions to ideas proposed by his managers in team meetings. In addition, Jack had done nothing to correct years of preferential promotion of male engineers in the manufacturing division.

The Vice President for Human Resources warned the C.O.O. that something had to be done. Jack's behavior was discouraging some of the company's best employees, and was giving Intertech a poor reputation that made it difficult to recruit promising female professionals. There might even be a lawsuit. The C.O.O. immediately met with Jack to discuss the problem. The C.O.O. was encouraged that during most of the two-hour meeting Jack listened, though he denied letting his feelings about women influence his leadership of the manufacturing division.

The next morning the C.O.O. enlisted the help of a female management consultant. She agreed to provide Jack with a good book on the subject of sexism in the workplace and to counsel him privately over the next two months on the causes and consequences of his attitudes. As the C.O.O. put it, "Let's make him over into an executive that even N.O.W. would nominate as manager of the year." He also met privately with each of the women who had complained about Jack to reassure them that action was being taken.

Seven months later the C.O.O. received a letter from a lawyer representing six female employees, naming Intertech as defendant in a class action suit of discrimination.

## Why We Violate This Commandment

What went wrong in the C.O.O.'s plan? Why didn't Jack change his behavior enough for the company to avoid the lawsuit? It's difficult to answer the second question without getting inside Jack. The answer to the first is certain—the plan failed because of the target for change. The C.O.O. opted to change Jack's attitude rather than his behavior. Instead of targeting what Jack did, he targeted Jack.

### Attitudes Look Like the Best Target

If someone has a "bad" attitude about something, we naturally conclude that a change in that attitude is called for. This rarely makes sense. The "bad" attitude is not the problem. The problem is the unacceptable behavior that attitude *may* be causing—and we emphasize the word "may" because not all negative attitudes lead to negative behavior. We have known managers, for example, who detested their bosses yet treated them with respect and performed their jobs marvelously. Even if their bosses knew about the low esteem in which they were held—and many of them didn't—they had no grounds for complaint. Insubordination exists in what people do, not in what they think. Notice that there are no laws against prejudice (thinking), only against discrimination (doing).

Another reason not to target attitudes for change is the enormity of the task. People spend lifetimes formulating and reinforcing values, beliefs, and principles—the stuff on which attitudes are based. What chance do we have of changing those convictions in one day, one week, one month, or even one year?

Finally, attitudes are *inside* us. As such, they represent a private side of our being. Attempts to modify them involve intrusion into our innermost fabric. This explains why most people become highly defensive and resist any attempt to change their attitudes.

## We Allow Ourselves to Get Angry

Difficult people try our patience. It is only human that determined resistance to our ideas frustrates and even angers us. However, these emotions may lead us to react to the person rather than respond to the behavior that is the real problem.

For two years a father had worried about how his son hopped from job to job, never settling down or moving up. He sat the young man down to talk about striving for what he wanted, whatever it was. It became clear that the son wasn't thinking beyond the present. The father was disappointed by what he saw as "lack of ambition," and his disappointment was exacerbated by how much his son meant to him. He exploded and called his son lazy and uncaring. Since the son certainly didn't intend to be as miserable as he was, he in turn became angry with his father for giving him so little credit. Naturally, the son rejected his father's criticism and advice.

Rather than focus on what his son could do to envision a future for himself, the angry father attacked his son's personality. If he had responded to the behavior that troubled him—his son's inability to articulate a future—he would have saved the family a lot of grief. He might have invited his son to spend a day picturing the future he desired. That task could have set the son on a forward path, given him a way to respond to his father's concerns, and preserved their good feelings.

## We Identify People Rather Than Behavior as the Problem

In one of our seminars we ask managers to raise their hands if they have ever encountered a problem performer. Typically, ninety percent or more of their hands will go up. Imagine their bewilderment when we say, "No, you haven't—no one in this room has ever seen a problem performer. They don't exist. There are no problem performers; there are only problem *performances.*"

This belief is critical for two reasons. First, it is the truth: people don't disappoint us, their behavior does. Second, it discourages us from attacking people and encourages us to attack the real culprit—behavior. Don't confuse cause and effect. "Poor performer" is simply a label we attach to someone who puts in a problem performance.

## We Mistakenly Attribute Intent to the Person

Did you ever notice how often you assume that people who behave in a troublesome way are doing it intentionally? There are at least two reasons why this assumption is wrong more often than right.

First, it gives people more credit for cleverness than they deserve. One of the authors had occasion to report to a group of vice presidents that many employees were convinced that their recent flurry of poorly considered changes had been a conspiracy to make life difficult. The executives broke out laughing. They explained that the last thing they were capable of was conspiratorial behavior—they were rarely capable of cooperating toward a common goal!

Second, relatively few people are as devious as we think. We are usually too quick to attribute evil intent to others. If you don't believe this, ask yourself how many times *you* have been wrongly accused by others of devious behavior.

## How to Implement This Commandment

The first imperative in transforming behavior is to minimize the threat that your request for change presents. The second is to concentrate your efforts on the action that you want, not on the person who will provide it. The prescriptions below are the best advice to follow in shaping new behavior in others without unduly raising their defenses.

### Target the Behavior for Change

What exactly is the problem? Are you certain it is a *behavior* that harms the organization, the other person, or your relationship, and not merely an *attitude* that you may need to learn to live with? What damage is being done? Is anything being violated other than your need to control the other person?

There's a simple test of whether you're addressing yourself to a behavior or an attitude: If you can't see it, it's an attitude. For it to be a behavior, you must be able to inspect it. Only when you can inspect what you expect will you start moving people.

In "The Sexist," the C.O.O. thought that Jack's prejudice against women was the problem—it wasn't. The problem was how Jack treated women. Instead of thinking, "How do I change the way Jack feels about women?" he should have wondered, "How do I get Jack to behave toward women the same say he behaves toward men?"

The C.O.O. should have confronted Jack with the specific behavior that was creating problems at Intertech. If the personalities involved allowed, he might have brought Jack together with some of the women, and perhaps men, who could give Jack specific examples of his past sexist behavior, along with explanations of the impact of that behavior. The consultant would have been an excellent choice as facilitator of such meetings. The C.O.O. could also have acted as facilitator if he remained impartial and if all parties trusted his motives.

### Let Behavior Change the Attitude

One of the most fundamental and irrefutable principles of human existence is demonstrated by this relationship:

## Attitudes ⟹ Behavior

In other words, our actions are shaped by who we are: our values, prejudices, and beliefs—in short, our attitudes. This is why people frequently make the mistake of attempting to change behavior by altering attitudes. They believe they are attacking the root of the problem. They *are,* but with little chance of success. As Abraham Lincoln said, "Human action can be modified to some extent, but human nature cannot be changed."

Instead of focusing on attitudes, therefore, we should concentrate on modifying human action: in this case, a specific problem behavior. It's difficult for people to do something new that seems contrary to their attitudes. But if the reason is compelling enough—such as being promoted, or not being fired—people usually give it a try. After that, their attitudes may never be the same.

Once we start behaving in a new way, it doesn't take long for our minds to get used to that new behavior. We see benefits we missed in our previous conduct. We realize that fears that kept us from changing were groundless or exaggerated. We receive feedback that enables us to refine the new behavior further, gaining more rewards. After a while (in our experience, only about twenty-one working days), our attitudes actually change to reflect what we've assimilated from the new behavior. In other words, the relationship shown above is more accurately presented as:

**Attitudes ⟺ Behavior**

---

Consider the case of people who don't use seat belts when they drive a car. If we were to offer these people $100 a day for three weeks to buckle up, they would probably take us up on the offer. By the end of that period, most of them would have gotten into the habit of buckling up when they entered a car, and therefore would continue to ride in safety. Furthermore, they'd feel more comfortable with the straps; their attitudes about seat belts would have changed.

Imagine if, instead, we invest $2,100 in psychotherapy for each of these drivers, to unearth their deep-rooted attitudes about seat belts. How many of them would be buckled up after three weeks, or ever?

Prejudices like Jack's are very difficult to erase, but modifying specific actions can produce amazing results. What if the C.O.O. had directed Jack to ask women for their opinions first at all staff meetings? Eventually, that behavior would become part of Jack's normal management style. Furthermore, the positive response—pleased female employees, good new ideas, and the C.O.O.'s praise—would change Jack's attitude about listening to women.

## Condemn Deeds, Not Doers

When you hate what is happening in your relationship with someone, say so—in a direct manner. Identify the behavior or performance that concerns you, but separate that behavior from the person. This minimizes defensiveness and feelings of punishment by others and will encourage them to listen to what you have to say.

One way to avoid condemning doers is to prevent the word "you" from appearing anywhere near the beginning of your criticism. If the C.O.O. said, "Jack, *you* are going to have to change your attitude toward women," he undoubtedly would get a negative response. That three-lettered word *you* would make Jack throw up defenses even before the end of the sentence.

A much better opening would be one that focuses on the sexist behavior: "Jack, I hear that several of the women in manufacturing feel they are being treated in a nonprofessional manner. Specifically, I understand that . . . " This approach immediately focuses both Jack and his boss on the behavioral problem to be solved.

To complete the condemnation of the deed, tell the person what is wrong with the behavior. Be as objective as you can in your description of the problem. If its impact is felt at work, the problem might be stated in terms of a goal not being met. If, on the other hand, the harm is being done to you, to your relationship, or to another person, state the rationale for change in these terms. The C.O.O. could have accomplished this by saying something like, "These perceptions have a negative impact on morale, which can be expected to translate into reduced performance."

## State Your Feelings Nonpunitively

Tell the person how you feel about what is happening. It strengthens your case and it increases the other person's understanding of the impact of his or her behavior. However, don't impose guilt on the person. Here are several tips for making a constructive statement of your feelings.

- Avoid sarcasm, accusation, or moralizing.
- Don't share your feelings in front of others; keep them private.
- Time your statement so that your listener is receptive—not angry, fearful, or upset.
- Give the person a chance to respond to your statement. *Ask* for a response.
- Avoid finality (e.g., "I'll never trust you again").
- Communicate your desire to help.
- Communicate your optimism about the person's ability to change. (Remember, all saints have a past, all sinners a future.)

The C.O.O. might have stated his feelings about Jack's sexist behavior as follows: "I'm very disappointed at this response to your first year of leadership, but I'm committed to working closely with you to turn this situation around."

## Contract for Improved Performance

Get a commitment for corrective action. But before you do, be certain you have the facts straight and that there isn't some good reason for what previously went on. Offer the chance to explain past behavior. Ask questions to uncover anything you may have misunderstood and get the other person's perception. Do not move the discussion to the point of corrective action until you are fully convinced that you know what's going on.

Once you test your understanding of the situation, you are ready to contract for improved performance. One method is to suggest the other person's action that you feel will bring about an improvement in performance or in your relationship. Better yet, ask the other person to suggest the remedy. For example, you might ask, "What do you believe will keep this from happening again?" The answer to this question should be a commitment to a repeated behavior.

One performance contract that the C.O.O. might have made with Jack would be to ask the women he works with to give him immediate, but private, feedback whenever he addressed them with disrespectful language. They would also praise him when they saw progress. His promise would be not to react defensively to such feedback. If the women fulfilled their part in the contract, it might not even take twenty-one repetitions of such feedback to cure Jack once and for all.

And what about *your* role in the situation? Fault rarely seems to limit itself to one person. In the 1600s the duc de La Rochefoucauld said, "If we had no faults, we should not take so much pleasure in noting those of others." Examine your own responsibility for what is going on and commit yourself to improved performance even before the other person asks for it. This willingness to support the new future you wish to create will encourage others to fulfill their contract with you.

The C.O.O. would have done well to end his conversation with something like: "Jack, I realize that I haven't done anything to help you deal with this challenge. I'd like to change that by giving you feedback whenever I have a chance to observe you interacting with women. And I want to serve as a resource anytime you need to talk about *any* problems you encounter in the human relations part of your job."

The contract-making process can be summarized through a simple ABC formula:

**A: Attend** to what the person is doing.

**B: Behaviorally** identify the problems created by it.

**C: Contract** for new behavior.

## The Essence of the Fourth Commandment

- Target the behavior for change.
- Let behavior change the attitude.
- Condemn deeds, not doers.
- State your feelings nonpunitively.
- Contract for improved performance.

*You will never turn a man-eating tiger into a vegetarian, but the tiger can be trained to refrain from eating his trainer. That the tiger may still* want *to eat the trainer is less important than the fact that he refrains from doing so.*

LYLE SUSSMAN

# 5

# Model the Behavior You Desire

*Never send contradictory signals. Mean what you say; say what you mean; do what you say. Words contradicted by actions are hollow. You move others by being totally consistent in what you ask them to do, as well as how you ask them to do it. Carefully examine the role you may be playing in unconsciously reinforcing the behavior you are trying to change. Don't reinforce the behavior by enabling the person to perpetuate it.*

## The Bad Example

Harvey was the senior maintenance engineer for a seven-hundred-bed hospital. He was in charge of a six-figure budget and a staff of sixty-five full-time and eight part-time employees. He was an "engineer's engineer." He could simply listen to a machine and tell you what was wrong with it and what parts were needed to fix it.

After Harvey was a year and a half on the job, the Vice President of Operations called in a consultant to see if something could be done about the morale in Harvey's department. Harvey's employees were bypassing the chain of command to complain about him. They were also starting to show high rates of absenteeism and turnover. The Vice President wanted to see if Harvey could be taught to handle people with the same skill he handled machines.

The consultant spent five full days on the project. He interviewed Harvey, interviewed his employees, and randomly observed his management style. After collecting and analyzing his data, the consultant submitted a report that included the following observations:

- Harvey must stop sending contradictory signals. He tells different people different things and then denies the contradictions when they are brought to his attention. *Example:* Two different employees were told to use different tools to fix the same part on the same piece of equipment.

■ Harvey should not expect his employees to do things that he himself is not prepared to do. *Example:* He should not ask his employees to find ways to save money for the hospital while he requisitions new carpeting for his office.

■ Harvey should realize that his style is preventing some of the behaviors he is trying to elicit from his subordinates. *Example:* The employees and Harvey concur that he ought to increase delegation and push decision making down the hierarchy. But after he delegates a job, he monitors much too closely and is too quick to place blame if the assignment isn't carried out exactly the way he envisioned it.

The last line of the report summarized the consultant's overall impression: Harvey is shooting himself in the foot and doesn't even know it. His employees pay much closer attention to what he is doing than to what he is saying.

## Why We Violate This Commandment

As consultants we often encounter managers who "shoot themselves in the foot." These people try to move others without realizing that their own behavior sends a contrary message. There are at least four factors that may result in the sending of contradictory messages or lead to behavior that enables another person to perpetuate a behavior you are trying to change.

## You May Be Seen as Deceitful

Yes, Virginia, there are people in this world who cannot be trusted. Every day we hear about, read about, or personally experience people who consciously try to deceive us. They tell us the check is in the mail when it is not; they extol the virtues of a product they know cannot perform up to the billing; they ingratiate themselves with false flattery—telling us things they think we want to believe but deep down we know to be false.

When confronted with their apparent discrepancy, hypocrisy, distortion, or outright lying, these people either rationalize and continue to distort, or come clean and apologize. In either case, they have lost some degree of credibility. We are less likely to believe them and less likely to be moved by them.

Are you seen as one of these people? If people feel you can't be believed, you won't move them. Your words and actions must be in synch. What you promise must be delivered. What you say must be supported with what you do. Your motives must be convincingly pure. You must manage from a "clean and open agenda."

## You May Be Unaware of Your Contradictory Signals

The consultant in the case presented above discussed his report with Harvey immediately after presenting it to the VP of Operations. Harvey's response to the report was similar to that of most people when told that their messages are inconsistent: "I can't believe I'm creating that degree of confusion. It never dawned on me that my messages were seen as that far removed from my actions."

Although there are those among us who are deceitful, experience convinces us that the vast majority of contradictory messages are sent by people who simply don't know better or aren't aware of their frustrating communication style.

Consider the following examples of the unconscious contradiction of stated messages:

- A manager states that all meetings will begin on time and then waits twelve minutes for stragglers to come in. *The unstated message:* "I'm not really serious about your need to be on time."

- A foreman admonishes his employees to refrain from spreading rumors, but shares company gossip with his cronies at lunch. *The unstated message:* "There's really nothing wrong with rumors."

- A supervisor announces to all her employees that an open door policy will take effect immediately; any employee can come into her office and discuss any issue. When employees do come into her office she stares out the window, continually checks her watch, and appears uncomfortable. *The unstated message:* "Don't bother me with your stupid problems."

You may have a noble heart and honest intentions and still send mixed signals—not because you're Machiavellian but because you unthinkingly contradict your stated messages. As Charles Kettering once said, "You can be sincere and still be stupid."

## Circumstances May Require You to Change Your Message

Change is inevitable. We once saw Russia as our enemy; McDonald's now sells Big Macs in Moscow. Magazine ads used to carry endorsements of sports figures extolling the benefits of smoking; now smoking is restricted in public spaces. Two paycheck marriages used to be the exception in our society; now they are the norm. When circumstances change drastically and unexpectedly, your actions and the messages supporting them change just as dramatically.

The problem that leads to violation of the Fifth Commandment occurs when you respond to change, but neglect to inform others of the new circumstances. All they see is that you've begun marching to a different beat. They can't hear the drum playing the new beat, so they respond with confusion, anger, and frustration. You're not wrong for changing; you're wrong for not communicating the reason for the change. In many cases the only difference between perceived hypocrisy and perceived reasonableness is information—information about why previous messages are no longer appropriate.

## You May Believe Words Are More Important Than Actions

During the debriefing session with the consultant, Harvey was surprised that his people questioned his intent. "But I know I told them that we had to save money and that I wanted to increase their responsibility. I said it in meetings and I even put it in written memos. I know that I communicated to them."

Yes, he communicated to them, but with messages much more powerful than words—his actions. Harvey believed that the only message he was communicating was coming out of his mouth and printed in his memos. He was wrong.

If you want to move people, make sure that your creed is reinforced by your deed. Marion Wade, founder of ServiceMaster, has put it this way: "If you don't live it, you don't believe it." To expand on this view: If people don't see you living it, talking about it won't help.

## How to Implement This Commandment

In order to model the behavior you desire from others, you first need to know what's inside of you. Then recognize the outward signals you send that work both against and in favor of getting what you want.

### Examine Your Motives and Goals

If you find your messages falling on deaf ears, and nothing you say seems to move people in the direction you intend, ask yourself these questions:

*Have I ever lied to this person in the past?* If so, you have your work cut out for you. Admit your error, beg forgiveness, and work doubly hard at satisfying this person.

*Is this person suspicious because previous requests like mine proved deceitful or manipulative?* Find out what was negative about the experience. Indicate specifically how your proposal and your intent is different.

*If I were the other person, would I believe me?* Do you always tell people the truth and provide them with full disclosure? Or do you sometimes need to deceive them and withhold information in order to protect yourself? Guess what: if the second sentence sometimes describes you, they probably see you as someone not to be trusted.

*If I am concealing information, why am I doing it?* Sometimes you can't tell the whole truth in support of your actions. (Examples: proprietary trade secrets, impending reorganizations, contractual negotiations.) If you must withhold information, make certain your reasons are legitimate. If you cannot divulge them, just say, "I cannot give you a reason that will make sense to you at this time. I simply have to ask you to trust that there's a good reason for this action, which will become clear later." When the good reason becomes public, remind them of the role it played in the earlier decision.

*Might the person be sorry later for agreeing to my request?* If so, rethink whether you want to make the request, or if you should warn the person about the possible negative outcomes. Once you lose credibility with one person, you lose your ability to move others. The people you influence are walking billboards for you.

---

The essence of moving people is credibility. If you don't have it, make sure that everything you do and say from this moment on establishes you as a trustworthy source.

## Stop Enabling the Behavior You're Trying to Change

How do you unknowingly reinforce the behavior you are trying to get others to change? Would an objective, third party observer analyzing your actions conclude that your verbal pleas for change are being shouted down by your nonverbal support of the status quo? The four "don'ts" below will help you to steer clear of such enabling behavior.

*Don't make empty threats.* Every threat you make must be backed by your *intent* to carry it out, the *resources* to carry it out, and the *action* you promised if the other person fails to respond. In other words, don't talk the walk unless you can walk the talk. (How many parents pass this test with their children?)

*Don't protect people from the consequences of their behavior.* For example, don't bail out an employee who has been caught stealing. The extenuating circumstances you may be responding to will not be acknowledged by other subordinates. They will see only the lack of teeth in company policy.

*Don't make excuses for problem behavior.* We seem to be losing some of the will in our society to hold people accountable for their behavior. Alcoholics are in pain; sexists don't really mean what they say; racists can't overcome the effects of their upbringing; thieves need the money; murderers and rapists had deprived childhoods. When we make excuses for unacceptable behavior, the perpetrator feels, "They're right; I'm *not* responsible for my actions." As the ads sponsored by A Drug Free America say, "There's only one thing to tell an addict: 'Get better or get out.' "

*Don't pick up after other people.* A mother and father insist that their two children, aged nine and eleven, clean up the toys strewn throughout the house before they go to bed. When they fail to comply, these wise parents don't take the toys back to their children's room, nor do they live in what passes as a Fisher-Price junkyard. Instead, each derelict toy has a sticker affixed to it, showing a date two weeks in the future, and goes into a "penalty box" in the garage, not to be retrieved until the end of its sentence. Very few toys are left out at night.

Examine your motives for picking up after, protecting, or making excuses for a difficult person in your life. Is it possible that you really don't want the person to change? Is it possible that you want to keep the person dependent on you? Is it possible that you enjoy playing the role of martyr or savior?

## Realize that Everything You Do Is a Signal

Role modeling may be your most powerful tool of influence. There are many people who have yet to encounter a positive role model, someone with solid values whom they can emulate; this is both a condemnation of our society and an advantage for you as you strive to inspire others. A second reason role modeling works is that sight is our number one means of gathering information. In fact, as much as eighty-five percent of the average person's storehouse of data came in through the eyes. This explains why someone once said, "People don't listen to you speak; they watch your feet." Finally, leaders are condemned to operating in a fishbowl. This means that the people who serve you are constantly looking at you and taking their lead from your actions.

Is it guaranteed that your example will produce the desired behavior from others? Of course not. But there is a negative guarantee in role modeling: if you do one thing and ask others to do the opposite, either they'll refuse to do as you ask or they'll be very upset. The ill will you generate from those who comply unhappily is at least as destructive as the performance you lose from outright noncompliance.

The best thing about role modeling as an instrument of change is that it is so easy. You simply show people by your behavior everything you want from them. And not only does it bring results, it feels good, too. So don't ask others to do without unless you sacrifice to the point of pain. Don't ask others to pitch in unless you give. Don't ask for responsibility unless your accountability is renowned. Don't ask for hard work unless you are a dynamo. Don't ask for emotional control unless you're as calm as a millpond.

### Realize that Everything You Say Is a Signal

What did you say yesterday? What are you saying today? What will you say tomorrow? Are there any inconsistencies across the three? If you change your policy, tell people why. Share the rationale for your abrupt turnaround.

Are you telling different people different things? If you are, and you have not told them why to their satisfaction, don't be surprised if your message falls on deaf ears.

Are you doing everything in your power to make sure that all signals you communicate are orchestrated into a clear, unequivocal message?

## The Essence of the Fifth Commandment

- Carefully examine your motives and goals.
- Stop enabling the behavior you're trying to change.
- Realize that everything you do is a signal.
- Realize that everything you say is a signal.

*How can you say to your neighbor, "Let me take the speck out of your eye," while the log is in your own eye?*

GOSPEL OF MATTHEW

# 6

# Adapt Your Approach to the Person

*Direct your attention to the behavior you want to change without concern for protecting your ego. Empower people to comply with your wishes by being kind to them, listening to them, acknowledging their feelings, addressing their needs, and admitting your blame. Be flexible and confident enough to respond to people according to their particular behavior.*

## The Rental Manager

Frank Rivera is the manager of a branch of a nation-wide car rental company located at a large metropolitan airport. He was unwinding in his office at 4:00 PM on a Friday after one of the busiest weeks his agency had ever experienced. By tomorrow there would not be a single car on his lot. He was glad he wouldn't be in the office to deal with frustrated callers and walk-ins who would have to be turned away.

Just then he heard muffled shouts out in the agency. His instincts and his exhaustion told him to ride out whatever storm was brewing right where he was. Besides, his assistant manager Debbie Shimada could handle it—or so he thought.

Within sixty seconds, Debbie was in his office unraveling this tale of woe. A customer, John Bell, had reserved a minivan to supplement the family car on a week's vacation to the beach. He planned for his two older children to rotate driving the van, which would transport a younger sibling and the friends that all three had invited along. He claimed that when he made the reservation with his travel club, he was assured that his 23-year-old twins were permitted to operate the van. However, two months ago the rental company issued a new policy that twenty-five was the minimum age for drivers. Frank knew that the travel club had been informed of the rules change, so it was not the agency's fault.

After several minutes of arguing with Debbie, Mr. Bell had exploded. That was the shouting Frank heard. Debbie responded in kind; she felt he deserved it for treating her disrespectfully. In her words: "He had no right to speak to me like that."

Frank was forced to enter the fray. He walked out onto the floor and told Mr. Bell he was sorry but nothing could be done. In response, he and Debbie were branded as incompetents, and worse. At first Frank was dumbstruck by the outburst, but as the tirade escalated, Frank began to defend himself, his employees, and the company. He loudly protested the verbal abuse of himself and his employee. A shouting match ensued. Mr. Bell stormed out of the office.

What went wrong? When Mr. Bell's needs weren't met, he exploded. Frank didn't know how to deal with someone in Mr. Bell's state. He wasn't trained in how to respond appropriately to various types of difficult people, especially when they are irate customers.

## Why We Violate This Commandment

Emotions ran high at Frank Rivera's car rental agency, making that an extreme but hardly unusual case. Even when people are calm, most of us have trouble understanding and communicating to different personalities. It's a natural human problem. Fortunately, humans are also excellent at overcoming difficulties once we recognize their roots. Here are the common reasons why, especially in tense situations, we ignore the differences in personality of other people.

## We Become Self-centered

When challenged by a difficult person, most of us retreat into ourselves looking for a defense and for a way to conquer the obstacle that person represents. We become highly self-centered just when we need to do the opposite. Much of Abraham Lincoln's success can be explained by his lack of self-centeredness. He once put it this way: "When I'm getting ready to reason with a man, I spend one third of the time thinking about myself—what I'm going to say—and two thirds thinking about him and what he is going to say."

## We Assume Everyone Is the Same

One of the great puzzles of human nature is our inability to respond to differences in others. Most of us claim that we're unique, but lump all others into the same few buckets. As a result we treat others pretty much the same, regardless of their uniqueness. We stereotype others at the same time that we want to be treated as individuals.

## Tough People are Tough to Deal With

Many of us have not had enough experience in confronting difficult behavior head on. Most of the people we have encountered were well-behaved, reasonable human beings. We never learned the skills necessary to handle people who fly off the handle, accuse us unfairly, refuse to be honest, or engage in other troublesome behaviors.

Luckily, since almost everybody has a breaking point, it's likely that the difficult person confronting you acts politely and rationally much of the time. If you can calm him or her down, you'll have a much easier time resolving the problem. And the first rule of soothing someone else is not to get upset yourself.

## We Have Fragile Egos

Some people report feeling hurt, insulted, or disappointed by others' behavior when, in fact, no other person has the ability to hurt you with their words or actions—short of attacking you physically. In order to be injured by the behavior of another, we have to cooperate. This cooperation is most likely when a person has low self-esteem or high insecurity. If this describes you, it will be very difficult for you to practice the actions suggested in this chapter. Starting today, commit yourself to a plan to fortify your self-confidence so that you can begin responding to difficult people from your brain rather than reacting to them from your stomach.

## How to Implement This Commandment

Three basic strategies are required in order to deal successfully with difficult behavior. First, concentrate on improving the behavior, not protecting your ego. Second, adopt unselfish attitudes; it may feel unnatural at first, but it will improve the results you get with almost any form of difficult behavior. Third, understand the causes of, and how best to respond to, the classic types of difficult people.

### Focus on Behavior—Not Your Ego

The people who "misbehave" in your eyes rarely do in their own. In other words, you may feel they are acting improperly toward you, but they rarely see it that way. The malicious intent which you may ascribe to them is often far from the truth. Most people feel justified in their behavior, no matter how outlandish or improper it appears. They rarely realize that you experience their behavior as aggression. By understanding this you will see the value of changing their overreactive behavior rather than defending yourself from a supposed personal attack.

To help insulate yourself from apparently malicious behavior, remember this apt aphorism: "Never attribute to malice that which can be explained by incompetence." In other words, give people credit for their stupidity. What looks and feels like an attempt to punish is more likely blatant insensitivity. Why feel harmed when no harm is intended? And if someone *is* trying to get under your skin, why give them the satisfaction of succeeding?

## Empower People to Change Their Difficult Behavior

Here are a number of tactics to use in the face of interpersonal disagreements. They work well with everyone, not just "difficult" people.

- *"Kill" with Kindness.* Treat everyone well regardless of how they treat you. Smile, be kind, and show a genuine interest in them and in their problems. Be direct, but likable and polite. It is difficult to treat a thoughtful person thoughtlessly.

- *Listen and Respond.* The Second Commandment in this book is "Listen Before Talking; Think Before Acting." Listening is essential for fixing any relationship problem. But listening alone is not enough; you must respond to what you hear. Wait until the other person has fully expressed his or her feelings. Then acknowledge your *awareness* of the situation, describe what you *see and hear,* reveal what you *think and feel,* and say what you *want.* Don't judge ("You shouldn't be that way") or generalize ("You always do that").

- *Acknowledge the Validity of All Feelings.* Often people whose behavior you want to change feel that the goal you're setting for them is beyond their grasp. For example, a manager who seeks to transfer greater responsibility to an employee might hear, "Oh, I don't think I'm ready to handle that. I don't understand the business well enough yet to perform up to your expectations in that job."

Many managers would respond with something like, "It's not as difficult as you think, and besides, I have great confidence in your ability to learn quickly. Give it a try." A thinking manager would instead acknowledge the validity of the employee's feelings and say something like, "Yes, it will be quite a challenge for you. But, I believe you're up to the challenge, and I'll be here to help you every step of the way."

■ *Don't Take a Position—Deal With a Need.* Positions are supposed to be solutions to needs. Frank Rivera got nowhere by sticking to his position of, "Company rules say that drivers under twenty-five may not operate the van," while John Bell insisted, "My children must be permitted to drive the van." Had Frank considered that Mr. Bell needed to get his whole family to the beach while making the twelve-hour drive alone with his wife, Frank might have looked for a solution they could both live with.

Usually there are several possible solutions for every need. Chances are that the difficult person confronting you has simply adopted the most obvious. It is your job to look beyond stated positions to people's motivating needs so that you can offer alternative ideas. In summary, move from *what* they want to *why* they want it.

- *Accept Blame.* More often than not you have played some role in bringing about the behavior others subject you to. What exactly is that role? Admit whatever your fault is quickly and emphatically. Whenever you shoulder your share of blame, others are more likely to own up to theirs. Sometimes you can encourage the other person to be cooperative by claiming even more responsibility than you deserve. Frank Rivera could have broken his customer's anger by loudly asserting, "You're right, Mr. Bell, we blew it. But that's in the past; now let's see what we can do to get us both out of this bind."

## Know the Different Types of Difficult People

Someone once said, "Never whisper to the deaf or wink at the blind." This wisdom tells us to know our audience, and to communicate to them in ways that are appropriate to them. This is especially important when someone is making your life difficult. The more you understand the motives behind a particular difficult behavior, the more likely you are to resolve it in a fashion consistent with your goals.

While it is impossible to neatly categorize each of the interpersonal challenges presented to us, it is useful to recognize certain behavioral patterns and to identify sensible responses to each one. Five especially frustrating patterns are described below, along with a few recommended responses. Their varied manifestations in the business milieu are presented in the Advisories found in the second half of this book, along with more precise advice.

**Rhinos** have a powerful need to have their own way. They like to tell you what to do. They resist your attempts to give them guidance or help them. Rhinos believe that rules were made for others to follow and them to ignore. Rhinos are controlling, aggressive, and sometimes hostile. They may even call you names, push your buttons, and engage you in emotional blackmail. An employee who challenges your authority, daring you to retaliate, is a Rhino.

Mistakes we make with Rhinos:

- We back off—they're counting on it.
- We go head on—they stampede us.
- We become flustered—they win.

What to Do with Rhinos:

1. Keep them in a nonaggressive physical position (e.g., sitting down).
2. Listen until they blow off steam and run out of things to say.
3. When they begin to wind down, jump in with an assertion of the needs to be met in this situation.

4. Don't let them interrupt. (Say, "I'm not through yet.")

5. Avoid the word "you," which sounds like a counterattack. Talk about "it," the behavior.

6. Startle them to get attention. "Everything you've said is right. Let me tell you exactly what I plan to do to get things back on track."

**Erupters** show spurts of Rhino behavior. Most of the time they pose no problem, but they are potentially explosive and can fly off the handle at the slightest provocation. John Bell, the customer in the car rental office, was an Erupter.

Mistakes we make with Erupters:

- We attempt to reason with them before they finish blowing off steam.

- We counterattack—they escalate.

- We accept their apologies afterward; we miss the opportunity to use the apology to gain a footing to propose a solution.

What to Do with Erupters:

1. Let them vent completely. Listen to them to gain their confidence and to position yourself to propose a solution.

2. Help them to regain composure before reasoning with them.

3. Empathize with their plight without necessarily admitting blame. Say, "I can see why you feel that way."

**4.** Respond actively and enthusiastically when it's your turn.

**5.** Address their concerns directly or they'll explode again.

**6.** When all else fails, say, "What is it you would like me to do?"

Frank Rivera was not prepared to handle an Erupter. He should have allowed Mr. Bell to shout his piece, thereby soothing his frustration and giving him confidence in the agency's desire to help. Then he could have empathized with Frank ("I can see why you wanted your children to drive the van. Let's see if there's anything we can do"), and offered his best solution. Allowing him to vent would have prevented the encounter from deteriorating as it did.

**Snakes** are Rhinos without the guts to fight openly. They sometimes stab you in the back. They make lots of critical or sarcastic remarks, but rarely in your presence. They may lie, deny their aggression, and often attribute their devious motives to others ("Guess what so-and-so is saying about you"). One example of a Snake is a competitive coworker who whispers sour nothings in your boss's ear about you.

Mistakes we make with Snakes:

- We don't confront them—they're counting on us to avoid a scene.

- We retaliate with the same dirty tricks—we look bad.

What to Do with Snakes:

1. Bring the aggression out into the open by confronting the Snake head on—"I know what you did."

2. Don't argue when the Snake denies intent to harm you.

3. Ask lots of questions to force the Snake's hand. "Why didn't you come to me with your concern?"

4. Insist upon the new behavior you want. "Next time I expect that you'll let *me* know exactly how you feel before you go to anyone else."

**Grouches** are picky people. They complain constantly. Their job is to point out faults and problems so you can correct them. They blame others for their mistakes and shortcomings. They are negative people who complain that the glass is half empty, and think it's your job to fill it. Grouches won't let you forget the mistakes of the past—both yours and theirs. A boss who looks for errors in employees' work with such relish that he rarely finds anything nice to say about their accomplishments is a Grouch.

Mistakes we make with Grouches:

- We agree with their valid complaints; that reinforces the invalid complaints, too.

- We tune them out and ignore them.

What to Do with Grouches:

1. Listen to them closely to make them feel important.
2. Make them be specific about their complaints. Force them to document who is involved, what has happened, where it exists, and why it is a problem.
3. Acknowledge what they've said without agreeing with it. "I see the problem you're identifying."
4. Get them to recommend a solution. "What have you done so far? How do you think it should be handled? If you *could* think of something to do, what would it be?"
5. Drag Grouches into the present and focus them on fixing the future. "Now that we have dealt with the past, let us both agree that as we search for a solution, we won't bring up anything that occurred more than an hour ago."
6. When Grouches are people that you serve (e.g., customers), ask them for a specific request you can fill.

**Do-nothings** promise everything and deliver nothing. They may be perfectionists who want everything to be just so before they'll act. Their procrastination may be linked to fear of failure, or even fear of success. Sometimes the Do-nothing is capable of accomplishing jobs that are fun, but simply cannot face unpleasant tasks and keeps postponing them. In other cases the Do-nothing has simply not been exposed to role models who follow through. An example of a Do-nothing would be a superior who won't make a decision on a request you've made because she fears the criticism it might bring.

Mistakes we make with Do-nothings:

- We leave it totally up to the Do-nothing to act.

- We accept their unrealistic commitments.

What to Do with Do-nothings:

1. Raise their level of discomfort by rejecting promises you don't believe they'll keep. "Actually, I'd prefer that you not promise to do it that quickly; but get it to me when it's done."

2. Maintain as much control as you can over the action.

3. Help them to remain task-oriented by defining the problem and structuring its solution in terms of specific goals and realistic deadlines.

4. Force yourself into the process at key points to keep it moving. "I'll be free at 3:15 PM this afternoon; where will you be? Good; call me then at extension 456 with your answer."

5. Confront procrastination and bring any related issues out in the open.

6. Praise them when they *are* decisive.

---

## The Essence of the Sixth Commandment

- Focus on behavior—not your ego.
- Empower people to change their difficult behavior.
- Know the different types of difficult people.

---

*What a man really means when he says that someone else can be persuaded by force is he himself is incapable of more rational means of communication.*

NORMAN COUSINS

---

# 7

# Provide for Dignity and Self-Respect

*We all have the need and the right to feel good about ourselves. When we violate this right, we fail to move others—or else we move them in unintended and unwanted directions. When people are belittled or degraded, they find ways to retaliate or sabotage our efforts.*

## The Critic

Sharon Calabrese was an achiever from the first day she entered kindergarten. Regardless of the assignment, she always had to be the first one done and receive the highest grade. This drive to excel carried all the way through her MBA degree from a prestigious university.

She brought the same intense work habits to her first job as regional operations manager for a national restaurant chain. She was thrilled with the job. It allowed her to use her ambition and competitiveness to expand her customer base, increase profits, and share in the corporate success she helped create.

At her first regional meeting she asked each of her seven managers to present a ten-minute overview of what their restaurants had done the preceding year and what their plans were for improving that performance during the next fiscal period.

None of the managers had ever received training in formal presentations, and Sharon did not provide any specific guidelines. The seven presentations covered the basics but lacked visual aids and contained none of the flourishes Sharon had grown to expect in her MBA program.

When all seven managers finished their presentations, she stood up and in slow, measured phrases told each of them what she thought of their performance. Three of the seven were roundly criticized together as follows: "I have never seen anything so unprofessional. I don't know what your previous boss told you, but from now on I expect you to give presentations that look as if you put some thought and planning into them. I heard better speeches when I was in high school. No manager in my region is going to make me look bad with the kind of amateur performances I just witnessed. If you can't take a simple assignment like this seriously, how can I trust your commitment to the really important aspects of your job?"

That night the seven managers met at the hotel bar to commiserate. They all felt that Sharon was way out of line in her critique of the three presentations. This rebuke, and several that followed, had laid the groundwork for significant alienation. In the words of Bob Franklin, one of the targeted managers, "It's gonna be a long time before I forget how she raked me over the coals. Mark my words—the day will come when she gets hers."

Over the next month Sharon drilled her managers in what she expected from them. Their next presentations showed dramatic improvement. Bob's presentation was the best of all, and revealed his deep understanding of the business. Sharon was pleased. Two months later Bob took a job with another chain and walked out of the restaurant he managed on the busiest day of the year.

## Why We Violate This Commandment

Almost no one sets out to denigrate another human being. Indeed, we usually criticize in order to help others improve their performance. However, we should never let good intentions make us blind to other people's psychological needs. Otherwise, our attempts to move people can easily rob them of their dignity and self-respect. There are many reasons why, but four are especially common and destructive.

### We Give Lip Service to the Golden Rule

There are certain guiding principles which are communicated to us almost from the moment we emerge from the womb. One of these principles is the Golden Rule: "Do unto others as you would have them do unto you."

In fact, one response we frequently hear about our management seminars is, "It seems as if you guys are talking about nothing more than the Golden Rule." Exactly! Most of the principles behind successful leadership or effective communication are extensions of that one profound axiom. Yet we violate that axiom every day in myriad ways. Many of us have a double standard; we are far more likely to notice if we don't receive respect than if we don't give it.

## We Don't Respect Ourselves

Abusers come in all shapes, sizes, and colors. They can be high school dropouts or they can hold advanced degrees. There is no demographic profile of the individual likely to inflict physical or psychological abuse. Yet there are characteristics which abusers seem to share. First, they have probably been abused themselves. Psychological counselors have a favorite saying: Show me someone who abuses and I'll show you someone who has been abused.

Second, abusers tend to have feelings of inadequacy, they don't feel good about themselves. People who lack self-respect are not likely to respect others. These are people who believe that since they don't deserve dignity and respect, no one else does either. They beat up on others because they've been beat up themselves.

## We Have an Inflated View of Our Own Importance

Abusive behavior can result when we have an abnormally low self-esteem, but also when we adore ourselves. As soon as we start believing our press clippings, we run the risk of assuming that we deserve special treatment from the "little people." Someone once said that the only little people are those who believe there are little people.

Sharon's demeanor was haughty and conceited. She wore her prestigious MBA as if it were a medal.

Can condescending tones and haughty airs influence people? Of course—it's done all the time. After all, the corporate Golden Rule is that those who have the gold make the rules. But you invariably run the risk of alienating the people whose ideas you have quashed—an alienation that will eventually return to haunt you. Samuel Butler once said, "He that complies against his will is of his own opinion still."

## We Think in the Short Term

When push comes to shove, most etiquette books get thrown out the window. Deep down, many of us believe that sensitivity toward others is fine as long as we have the time and the other party is being cooperative. But when there is pressure or opposition, consideration may seem to be a disposable luxury.

This knee-jerk reaction indicates a desire for immediate victory. We fail to consider how inconsiderate behavior now will affect future transactions with this person. We fail to realize that victory at the expense of the other party's self-esteem lays the groundwork for eventual defeat. We win the battle, but will eventually lose the war.

Sharon was an achiever who expected others to perform as well under pressure as she did. In her attempts to get her people up to speed overnight, she was looking for quick gain. Sharon made her point; their speeches improved rapidly. But she also got something she didn't bargain for when one of her best managers quit.

## How to Implement This Commandment

It's easy to resolve to treat others as you want to be treated. But it's also easy to neglect that rule when you're in the middle of an argument or focused on a task. The key to following the Seventh Commandment of Change is to prepare yourself mentally. Lay the groundwork for your next encounter by taking these steps.

### Examine the Roots of Your Dignity-Robbing Behavior

Are you reflecting the abuse you've received at the hands of others? If so, recognize that you aren't destined to perpetuate the treatment you received, nor do you have to remain a slave to it. The abuse you received from others said much more about them than it does about you. Realize that no one has the right to abuse you physically or psychologically; nor do you have the right to abuse another. Realize that you should never passively accept abuse from another on the assumption that it is somehow "deserved." You have the option of living your life in a destructive fashion, abusing yourself and others. Or you can maintain your dignity while allowing others to maintain theirs. Which option do you choose?

Do you think, like Sharon, you're pretty hot stuff, generally unmatched in ability by the people around you? It may sound strange, but this is another form of low self-esteem. People who really feel satisfied with themselves have no need to put down other people. They criticize behavior when necessary, but always stop short of attacking personalities and stealing dignity. If, like Sharon's managers, the people you correct often feel devastated, clean up your act. You and she are *not* better than they are. Sharon may be schooled in the fine points of making presentations, but after a few hours of instruction her managers will be right where she is. And they have undoubtedly mastered many tricks of the food industry that she needs to learn.

## View Others as Integral to Your Success

Whenever you ask anyone to do anything, you do so to make your life easier. Thus, you really depend on other people to help you achieve a personal goal. Fortunately, one of the most basic of human needs is to feel valuable, to help others. So when you want to move others, communicate that you need them. It will help your cause, while at the same time uplifting them.

Convince people that:

- You need them
- Your success is directly dependent upon their success
- You realize how important they are to achieving your goal
- There are no "little people" on your team

You can tell people these things, but how do you convince them? Believe these points yourself!

Paul "Bear" Bryant, the famous University of Alabama football coach, said: "When we win a football game, *they* did it; when we tie a game, *we* did it; when we lose a game, *I* did it. That's all it takes to win football games."

One of the standard definitions of management is achieving results through the efforts of others. You achieve because of those who work with and for you. If you don't believe this, or fail to make it clear to everyone who'll listen, you won't move others.

## Allow Others to Save Face

Psychologists tell us that we all need to feel good about ourselves. We want to be able to hold our head high. Face-saving is nothing more than allowing people to maintain their dignity when it is threatened. Here are six suggestions for letting people preserve their self-esteem:

1. Don't demand or command; request. People want to believe they are acting out of their own free will, not out of yours. The best salespeople in the world don't sell anything. They get people to buy by having them see how much they will gain from the product. None of us wants to be sold, but all of us want to gain.

2. Criticize privately. Share constructive criticism face to face, without onlookers— not as Sharon did in full view of peers.

3. Don't talk at or to people; talk with them. Don't use a condescending, demeaning tone.

Get off your pedestal and listen to others. You are less threatening when you show your own vulnerability and foibles. Laugh at yourself. For example, Sharon could have told her managers that she used to be terrified of giving speeches until someone showed her how to do it and enjoy it.

4. Attend carefully to nonverbal cues. When you detect that others are uncomfortable, slow down, pull back, and allow them to talk. Are they becoming agitated or tense? Are they breaking eye contact? Are they clenching their fists or stiffening their bodies? If the answer to any of these questions is yes, it may be time for you to provide face-saving. They are feeling a threat to their self-esteem which you must recognize and respond to immediately.

5. Anticipate the need for face-saving whenever others are clearly giving something up to make the change you request. For example, if you have just resolved a conflict between two employees, one of them may appear to be the "loser." Take that person aside immediately to offer your thanks for the sacrifice you know was made.

6. Finally, learn from the masters of face-saving: the Japanese. Never offend knowingly, and always seek forgiveness. If you feel that apologizing is a sign of weakness, ask yourself these two questions: When a boss or parent admitted to you that he or she had made a

mistake, did you see it as a sign of weakness or as a sign of strength? Did the apology make you feel that you wanted to do less for that person or more?

## Treat People as if They're Special— They Are

We all want to feel that we are special, more than just one among five billion earthlings. Most of us believe that others ought to be treated as special, too. But what exactly does that look like and sound like? How can you do it as you convince others to change? You show others they are special when you:

- Listen to them, giving value to their ideas. (See the Second Commandment.)

- Acknowledge the validity of their position from their perspective. Take the time to see the argument through their eyes, and feel it through their emotions.

- Speak in words they understand, and through examples that are real to them. Communicate to express, not to impress. But be careful not to condescend.

- Focus on them, to the exclusion of other potential distractions. Comfort them with the knowledge that they have your undivided attention.

- Don't stereotype people or categorize them as representative of a larger classification. Act as if there is no one else in the world exactly like this human being. This shouldn't be hard, because it's true.

- Empathize with them. Walk a mile in their moccasins, wing tips, heels, or running shoes. Ask yourself how you would feel if you were sitting on the other side of the desk.
- Remember their names and things important to them: their anniversary dates of hire, the courses they're taking, their birthdays, their children's names, their favorite pastimes, the nice things they said about you the last time you were together, the nice things someone else said about them (which you may now be sharing with them).

We live in a society and time where baked potatoes can be cooked in ninety seconds, messages can be sent around the world in an instant, and relationships are becoming increasingly transient. In this era, people are seeking affirmation of their uniqueness, dignity, and value. When you affirm these needs, you are more likely to move people. When you violate these needs, you pay the consequences.

## The Essence of the Seventh Commandment

- Examine the roots of your dignity-robbing behavior.
- View others as integral to your success.

- Allow others to save face.
- Treat people as if they're special—they are.

---

*The art of managing people is stepping on their toes without messing up their shine.*

ANONYMOUS

# 8

# Appeal to Self-Interest

*Provide reasons for changing that make sense to the person you are trying to change. How will the person benefit from adopting your position? What are the costs or consequences of not changing? People move when they believe it is in their best interest to move. Failure to appeal to their self-interest will result in failure to influence them.*

## The Low-Tech Manager

Peter Meyers was a forty-five year old sales manager for a large sportswear manufacturer. He started with the company immediately out of college and over the next twenty-four years worked his way up the corporate ladder. His duties included managing seventeen sales reps, developing sales forecasts, hiring and training, and personally supervising the largest retail accounts. The work was demanding, but he loved the challenge of managing people, sales, and customers.

His duties required analyzing significant amounts of information. As a matter of fact, Peter prided himself on being able to "read faster, listen better, and work a calculator quicker than anyone else in the company."

When personal computers were introduced in the company, Peter was openly hostile; he avoided training sessions and refused to have this "high-tech nightmare," as he called it, put in his office. When his boss questioned his aversion to the computer, Peter said, "I've handled this job without complaints for the past five years. Why should I have to develop computer skills to perform a job that I'm already performing well? Besides, gadgets and I don't mix. Microchips intimidate the hell out of me. If God wanted us to be computer literate, he would have given us computer chips for brains."

Peter's boss tried a variety of strategies to get Peter "on-line." He asked politely. Peter refused politely. He had the computer hooked up in Peter's office when Peter was out of town. Peter never turned it on. He enlisted Peter's closest friends in the company to point out the folly of his resistance. Peter ridiculed their efforts.

The boss finally called him into his office and said, "Peter, I can't put up with your resistance any longer. You have a nineteenth-century mentality in a twenty-first-century world. You have two choices: learn to use the computer in two weeks or look for another job."

Fourteen days later, having discovered no compelling reason to become computer-literate, Peter Meyers submitted his resignation.

## Why We Violate This Commandment

Almost everybody sees the logic of appealing to the self-interest of others to convince them to move. Yet we see managers breaking this Commandment all the time, and becoming frustrated as a result. The majority of violations can be attributed to one or more of the following causes.

## We Think Resistance to Change Is the Problem

Had you asked Peter's boss to describe his dilemma, he would probably have said something like, "Peter is resisting our conversion to computers. He won't be moved." That's not a useful statement of the problem. The real issue is that Peter's boss couldn't find a way—or didn't try to find a way—to make it in Peter's best interest to accept the computer.

One of the primary reasons we fail to move others is that we define the situation inaccurately. We see someone resisting our attempt to move them. This view results in significantly different consequences from one which focuses on the other person's needs. The problem is not the other person's resistance. The real problem is your failure to challenge that person's need to hang on to the past. Peter never accepted his boss's assertion that logging onto the computer was in his best interest—probably because the boss never wondered, "Now let's see; how will Peter benefit from using the computer?"

Your problem in getting others to change is not that they refuse to move. Your problem is that you have yet to figure out how to make movement appear to be in the other person's best interest.

## We Focus on What People Want, Not Why They Want It

Peter said that he didn't want to use a computer. That was his position. But there were reasons why he resisted—reasons which apparently were never explored in discussions with his boss. If his boss had probed the reasons behind Peter's opposition, he might have found the "carrot" to move Peter. Had he been a good listener, he would have understood the fears that automation evoked in Peter.

Focusing on what people want rather than on why they want it necessarily creates problems for us and for the people we're trying to move. We're likely to get angry and frustrated because what we want is not what they want. And we get angrier when we assume that they're stupid and obstinate for wanting what they want. Then everyone "digs in." When people attack our position, the natural tendency is to become even more entrenched. After all, how many of us want to lose face by having to admit that our stand may not be as valid as we thought it was?

Focusing on the position rather than the rationale behind it quickly moves the situation from a potential win-win to a win-lose or, even worse, a lose-lose situation. Rather than looking at the situation as one where we can both walk away ahead, we are likely to regress to a view that one or the other party must lose.

Peter resigned rather than learn how to use the computer. He lost a job he loved. His boss focused solely on positions, put an ultimatum on the table, and lost a valuable sales manager with twenty-four years of experience in the company.

## We Don't Know How to Appeal to Self-Interest

It's one thing to appreciate the importance of appealing to another's self-interest. It's quite another to know how to do it.

When Peter's boss gave him an ultimatum, he obviously did it as a last resort, thinking that Peter would come to his senses (from the boss's perspective). Whenever we draw a line with someone, we do it out of frustration and a feeling of helplessness. We believe that we're out of options, and we don't know what else to do.

Deep down, most of us realize that there probably is a way to move the person other than a win-lose or lose-lose option, but we don't know what it is. We know intuitively that an appeal to the other person's self-interest makes good sense. But how do you do it?

## How to Implement This Commandment

There are five basic strategies for appealing to the other person's self-interest. Try them, and see how much easier your work becomes.

### Tune In to "Station WII-FM"

Assume for a moment that the other person is communicating to you via radio frequency. If you really want to apply the Eighth Commandment, the first thing you must do is tune into station WII-FM— "What's In It—For Me?"

Develop a new frame of mind when you're about to move someone. Instead of focusing on what you're trying to get them to do, start focusing on what's in it for them if they do it. Focus on the benefits they'll derive, the advantages they'll experience.

You tune into WII-FM when you:

- Look at the situation through their eyes, not your eyes.

- Realize that from their perspective resistance is neither irrational nor a sign of obstinacy. There are reasons why they are not moving, reasons which make eminently good sense to them.

- Realize that your desire to move the other person may not be any stronger than the other person's desire to maintain the status quo.

## Recognize the Needs that Motivate People

The question: "What moves people?" has generated heated debate since the first pharaoh hired the first management consultant to help speed up construction of his pyramid. Within the last fifty years social psychologists and management theorists have adopted widely accepted answers to this question. Regardless of our age, sex, religion, or socioeconomic class, we all have needs for:

*Sustenance:* Food, water, shelter, and other physical comforts

*Safety:* Protection from injury, illness, death, financial disaster, layoff, and arbitrary treatment

*Society:* Affiliation, camaraderie, social support, love

*Self-Esteem:* Feeling good about ourselves;

maintaining positive self-regard through opportunity for accomplishment, recognition, growth, creativity, challenge, enjoyment, involvement, ownership, and independence

*Self-Actualization:* Achieving our fullest potential; becoming all we can be; accomplishing our ultimate goals

*Spiritual Harmony:* Maintaining a comforting and strengthening belief system; matching our beliefs to our behaviors; achieving harmony among our various beliefs

Social psychologists have provided us with principles for using this set of needs in moving others. These principles teach us important lessons.

1. Not all needs are equally dominant at the same time for any individual. As our situation changes, so does the intensity of our needs. This explains why any two people whom you are trying to move are likely to respond to different appeals.

2. The most basic needs for sustenance and safety are usually fulfilled most of the time. Aside from the homeless and chronically unemployed, most of us have a roof over our head, clothes on our back, and food in our stomach.

3. The same "carrot" can fulfill several needs at once. For example, a salary increase may

enhance our self-esteem, allow us to socialize more with our friends, and help us satisfy the need for security by providing for retirement.

4. Self-actualization varies from individual to individual. For some, self-actualization may mean running a marathon in under three hours; for others it means raising a family of responsible children; for others it means getting their picture on the cover of *Fortune*.

5. We all have the same needs, but we don't all feel them at the same time, with the same potency, or in exactly the same way. If we were all exactly alike, Baskin and Robbins would only serve vanilla. That's why smart managers know their people as individuals, not as "subordinates," "sales clerks," or "machine operators."

## Help the Other Person Fill Important Needs

Whenever your attempt to move someone is frustrated by the person's resistance, change your perspective of the situation by asking different questions:

- Instead of asking why the person is obstinate, ask what needs are being fulfilled by resisting.

- Instead of asking why the person is unreasonable, ask what needs you should appeal to in order to move the person.

- Instead of asking the person, "What do you want?" ask, "Why do you want it?"

- Instead of asking the person *what* is objectionable in your proposal, ask *why* it is objectionable.

- Instead of thinking, "What should I say?" think, "What should I ask?"

- Instead of asking other people, "How can I overcome this person's resistance?" ask them, "What needs are motivating this person?"

- Instead of asking, "How can I sell this person?" ask yourself, "How can I help him or her?"

- Instead of asking, "Why are you resisting?" ask, "What would it take to make you happy?" (In the case of Peter Meyers: "What would enable you to feel good about switching over to a PC?")

With each of the suggested questions you are moving from a focus on what you want and why you want it to a focus on what the other person wants and why he or she wants it.

## Don't Fight Needs; Respond to Them

The oriental martial arts are all based on a common principle: Don't fight force with force—use your opponents' force against them. Apply the wisdom of this philosophy to your attempts to move others: don't fight the other person's needs—use them.

For example, if his boss had noticed Peter's strong need for self-esteem, he could have:

- Conceded that many managers with Peter's years of successful experience hesitate to move their work "on line," and that his skepticism is not irrational.
- Emphasized how computer literacy would add to his repertoire of skills as a sales manager.
- Demonstrated how spreadsheet software would enhance his decision-making ability.
- Suggested that Peter's influence in the company would increase substantially once he got on the computer network.

## Use Ultimatums Only as a Last Resort

This Eighth Commandment says that people will change when they see change as in their best interest. To the extent that avoiding discomfort is in our best interest, it follows that threats do represent a strategy for implementing this commandment: "Do it or you will be fired/reprimanded/demoted/reassigned/fined." There is some wisdom to Al Capone's quip that, "You can get more done with a smile and a gun than you can with a smile alone."

However, don't opt for the "gun" until you have given a "smile" every opportunity to work. Be certain you've explored all other options and have rationally concluded that an ultimatum is the last card you have to play. Use it only as a last resort, because chances are excellent that you won't be pleased with the results. Peter's boss certainly wasn't. Neither are many employees who threaten to quit if their demands aren't met.

## The Essence of the Eighth Commandment

- Tune in to station WII-FM.
- Recognize the needs that motivate people.
- Help the other person fill important needs.
- Don't fight needs; respond to them.
- Use ultimatums only as a last resort.

*People don't care how much you know until they know how much you care.*

ANONYMOUS

# 9

# Rejoice at Success

*Be happy when other people change in response to your needs. Don't allow your sense of entitlement to prevent you from rejoicing at their success. Look for opportunities to acknowledge the improvements of others. Look for the good before you look for the bad. When you find it, praise performances more than you praise people. Say how you feel about their efforts, and thank them.*

### The Ungrateful Manager

Robin Waitley is Human Resource Manager for the southeastern division of a pharmaceuticals firm. Her secretary of one year—Jennifer Taylor—had come highly recommended by her teachers, and proved to be a bright and talented assistant. She made very few mistakes and generally exercised good judgment. Nevertheless, her inexperience showed, occasionally requiring Robin to redirect her behavior.

Unfortunately, Jennifer rarely accepted the feedback in the spirit with which it was provided. She often became defensive, leading sometimes to tears, sometimes to withdrawal, and recently to angry outbursts. Robin, in turn, became tense about voicing any complaints.

Robin suspected that part of the problem might rest in the way she criticized Jennifer's work, so she attended a seminar on constructive criticism. Based on what she learned there, she became careful to condemn behavior and not Jennifer. She gave criticism as soon as possible after the problem performance, always in private, and never in anger. She offered plenty of examples, and she made positive suggestions for improvement. And her new methods were working!

Only yesterday Robin got a completely cooperative response from Jennifer in her quarterly performance review. In the past, one or two of her requests would have caused a visibly negative response, but not this time. Jennifer listened, voiced one disagreement in a respectful tone, pledged to fulfill her contracts for improved performance, and restrained herself mightily from becoming defensive.

Robin noted Jennifer's acquiescence in disbelief, waiting for the other shoe to drop, but it never did. Robin was still skeptical by the end of the review, and so withheld any outward sign of relief or appreciation. Her final comment to Jennifer was, "Okay, it sounds like we have the basis for a mutually beneficial working relationship, and I'm looking forward to the future." That night Robin realized, as she felt more relaxed than in a long time, that she really was looking forward to the next few months.

But at dinner that night, Jennifer expressed her feelings to her husband in this way: "After the effort I made to just sit there and agree to work on everything she asked for, she didn't even have the decency to thank me."

Robin blew the chance to acknowledge, reward, and thereby reinforce the behavior Jennifer had worked so hard to give her. Jennifer never did follow through on her promises to improve.

## Why We Violate This Commandment

One of the most glaring weaknesses in our relationships with others is our failure to give them what they feel is due credit for their efforts. Very few of the reasons for this failure are good ones.

### We Adopt a Wait-and-See Attitude

It is natural to be suspicious when people comply with your wishes—are your efforts really working? Some people cooperate only to get something in return. Others are genuinely motivated, yet backslide to their old ways. So our reaction to initial compliance is usually not to acknowledge their effort, for it may prove to be contrived or temporary. How foolish this is! No matter what the motive for changing a behavior, that behavior repeated often enough will bring about a new attitude. And what surer way is there to get a person to repeat a behavior than to praise it?

### We Feel Entitled to the New Behavior

Often the behavior we ask from others is what we feel they should have been doing all along. For example, we expect a subordinate to listen to our criticism and act on it willingly: should we therefore praise that employee for merely accepting and responding to our redirection? Praising someone for "only" doing their job is not something we normally do. But it greatly encourages future efforts.

## We Don't Understand the Power of Praise

Most human beings want to feel accepted, valued, and worthwhile. They want approval from others—especially those whom they respect. Praise is perhaps the supreme interpersonal motivator. Yet too few bosses, parents, and teachers seem to recognize the power of praise. Even though they desperately want their own accomplishments to be acknowledged, they fail to empathize with the very same need in others.

## We Are Uncomfortable Giving Praise

When you acknowledge someone's hard work, you reach out to that person, often in a warm and effusive way. But we've met hundreds of managers who have difficulty being so intimate with others. Some suffer from an impersonal upbringing: a manager in one of our seminars blamed his "praise-miser" behavior on parents who never said "thank you" to each other. Others have personality attributes or value patterns that prohibit expressing appreciation. For example, some people are absolutely convinced that the stick is more motivating than the carrot.

## We Qualify or Negate Praise

The assistant manager of a resort hotel in the Caribbean had been frustrated for months in his attempts to have the hotel beach combed every morning before the tourists came out to lie in the sun. Finally his efforts took hold: the seaweed was collected by 9:00 AM two days in a row. As the job was finished and the worker came off the beach, the manager wisely said, "Excellent job, Jim. That beach looks so good, I'm tempted to put on my bathing suit and get out there myself." Unfortunately, he added, "I only wish you had done it that way all summer."

Never negate or qualify in any way the praise that you give to someone who is finally cooperating. Whenever you do this, the good you accomplish with your praise is more than erased by the qualification. Certainly the young man who cleaned the beach feels, "I'll never be able to satisfy my boss!"

The best way to avoid the danger of negating praise is to never add anything to it. Nothing more is necessary. Even adding "Keep up the good work" is at best neutral, and does not enhance praise in any way. It may be seen as applying pressure for more improvement.

## How to Implement This Commandment

Always be on the lookout for success in others. Look for the good in others before you allow yourself to observe their faults. Search for evidence of the new performance you're looking for, and eventually you'll rejoice in the demise of their old counterproductive ways.

### Anticipate Opportunities to Praise

Those of us who are not ready givers of praise must prepare ourselves for the event. We have to be ready to respond positively to the behavior we're looking for or we may miss the opportunity to praise. This anticipation is difficult to accomplish because it must occur *before* the other person has begun to perform in the desired way.

You can see in "The Ungrateful Manager" how unlikely it was that Robin Waitley, in the middle of her frustration with Jennifer, would pause and ask herself, "Now let's see—how am I going to respond to Jennifer when she learns how to accept my criticism without defensiveness?" Yet this is precisely what Robin should have done. Had she acknowledged and reinforced Jennifer's progress when it occurred, Jennifer's newfound behavior would have begun to harden like newly poured cement under a warm sun. Instead, Robin rained on it.

The easiest way to implement this principle is to practice the famous advice offered in *The One-Minute Manager*. There we were told to devote our time to catching employees in the act of doing something *right*.

In your relationships with others, whether at work or at home, make it your goal to uncover victories, not to reveal screwups or dredge up past failures. If you look for the bad in others, you'll find it. If you look for the good, you'll find that. And if you find the bad first and deal with it appropriately, you're unlikely to be in the mood for giving out awards. No, you must have the awards ceremony first—there will be plenty of time and determination left to find and respond to any remaining problems.

### Praise the Behavior—Not the Person

As part of the Fourth Commandment we repeated for you a familiar, basic principle of constructive criticism: "Condemn deeds, not doers." What you may not have heard before is that this very same prescription applies to the giving of praise: *Praise deeds, not doers."*

To understand why this principle is so important to the giving of praise, consider this scenario. Imagine that at the end of the performance review Robin had responded in the following way: "Jennifer, you have justified my decision to hire you. You have turned out so well. Your contribution to the success of this office is more than I could have hoped for. I wish I had another dozen like you."

In fact, you might like to hear something like this from your boss. But on reflection there is a great deal wrong with such praise. First, it provides Jennifer with no clue as to what she is doing so well that pleases her boss. It does not empower her to continue doing what has earned raves from her boss. Second, it inflates Jennifer. Should Robin follow this with criticism anytime soon, Jennifer is likely to feel, "Yesterday I was a queen, and today I'm dirt." Third, it will reinforce the dysfunctional behavior of some employees with low self-esteem who hungrily search for pats on the back—quick fixes that don't satisfy their "habit" for very long. Direct your praise to *what* people have done right; it will please them just as much, and be effective in the long term as well.

### Say How You Feel About the New Behavior

While your praise should focus on the new performance, you also owe people a description of how the behavior makes you feel. This is the best way to let them know just how important it is for them to continue performing so well.

You don't need to say much: remember that the best way to avoid the danger of negating praise, which we talked about earlier, is to close your mouth as soon as you finish. Just two words, when uttered in a soft and sincere tone, will express your feelings perfectly. Those two words are, of course, "Thank you."

Had Robin Waitley applied the prescriptions of this commandment to the performance review, she would have responded to Jennifer's behavior in this way: "Jennifer, this has been our most productive feedback session. I am really pleased to have had the opportunity to tell you exactly how I feel how about your performance—most of which is exceptional—and that you are so cooperative in wanting to make the improvements we discussed. Your willingness to work on your telephone answering skills is especially helpful to me. Thank you."

## The Essence of the Ninth Commandment

- Anticipate opportunities to praise.
- Praise the behavior—not the person.
- Say how you feel about the new behavior.

---

*The deepest principle of* Human Nature *is the craving to be appreciated.*

WILLIAM JAMES

---

# 10

## Cut Your Losses with Remorse, Not Guilt

*Have realistic expectations of what you can accomplish in changing the behavior of others. Don't accept guilt for the failings of other people; instead, leave the responsibility for change with them. Give them enough time to change, but if they don't, distance yourself mentally and physically.*

## The Caring Friend

Charlene Edmonds is a social studies teacher at the West End Middle School. She is a dedicated, high achieving professional who has earned several awards for excellent teaching throughout her career. She loves working with students, has good rapport with parents, and maintains a productive relationship with the school principal and other district administrators.

Charlene's closest friend, Silvia Franke, is equally committed to her profession. Although she has yet to be publicly recognized for her work, students love her and parents appreciate her influence on their children. But, unlike Charlene, Silvia never has a kind word to say about her superiors—not the principal, the district superintendent, nor *any* administrator.

Silvia is one of the more militant leaders of the teacher's union, and is predictably out front in nearly every action they take in opposition to school administration and the school board. She is also free with criticism of management with anyone who will listen—even students and their parents. Her antagonistic relationship with superiors has been one of the few sore spots in the otherwise close friendship between Silvia and Charlene.

Silvia's behavior troubles Charlene for two reasons. The first is that Charlene respects the very same people that Silvia abhors; she finds it difficult to listen to Silvia's incessant complaints, which Charlene often believes to be unjustified. Her other concern is for Silvia's career. Charlene is absolutely convinced that Silvia, more than any other teacher in the district, would make an outstanding principal—a position she knows Silvia secretly covets. But as long as she continues her anti-administration behavior, she'll never be considered for such a promotion.

For years Charlene has pleaded with Silvia to amend her ways—both for Silvia's sake and to reduce Charlene's discomfort in their relationship. And she's still at it. She likes Silvia too much to give up, and her discomfort is too great to ignore the situation. Besides, she feels that as Silvia's best friend she could have done more over the years to help. Many times she passed up opportunities to point out how Silvia's behavior was hurting her career (or hurting Charlene), but never said anything. Keeping the peace in their relationship usually came first.

Several of Charlene's associates have advised her to accept that Silvia's behavior is beyond her influence, but Charlene stubbornly persists. The result is that Silvia is getting fed up with her "meddling." As of late she has been avoiding Charlene. In fact, Silvia would no longer identify Charlene as a valued friend.

## Why We Violate This Commandment

Why didn't Charlene know when to quit? Unfortunately, she was victimized by guilt, and her persistence made her friendship with Silvia suffer. What keeps people from cutting their losses?

### We Fall Victim to Co-dependence

Clearly, Charlene had become a co-dependent of Silvia. She began to see herself as partly to blame for Silvia's problem behavior. This guilt was part of the motivation behind Charlene's persistent attempts to reform her. As long as she felt some of the responsibility for what was going on, it was not possible for her to "bail out" on her friend.

The irony of co-dependence is that the responsibility we feel for the other person gets in the way of our being helpful. We don't give people the space they need to make their own decisions and solve their own problems. We also hang on long after we should, failing to protect our emotions from someone who has no intention of pleasing us.

### We Overestimate Our Influence

Everyone is self-centered to some degree. Those of us who are more highly afflicted believe we play a far more significant role in the lives of others than we really do. Other people may like us, respect us, even love us, but they also have independent minds and unique needs and values. While we may influence their attitudes and choices, ultimately they are going to make their own decisions—as they should.

Don't fall into the trap of thinking, "She loves me, so I'm sure she'll eventually see it my way." The way people think and therefore behave is not dictated by whom they love, admire, or respect. Influenced, yes; dictated, no. You may not succeed in changing the behavior of even the closest people in your life.

## We Can't Accept Defeat

One of the most wonderful human qualities is persistence. The most successful people in the world share this enviable quality. However, in dealing with people we have to learn when we have more to lose than to gain by sticking to our guns.

The time to stop trying usually coincides with either of two events. One is when the other person asks you to. When someone sits you down and says, "Look, I want you off my back," that person usually means it. Comply. Alternatively, it is time to give up your crusade when it becomes apparent, even without the person asking you to back down, that your relationship will suffer permanent damage in the name of help. Charlene's inability to read such writing on the wall cost her Silvia's friendship.

Stubbornness may be admirable in many phases of life, but not when the damage we are doing outweighs any potential gain.

## How to Implement This Commandment

It takes time and effort to move a person to new behavior. With the guidelines that follow, you can develop a good sense of how long and how far you can push a person. Eventually, should your endeavors not succeed, you will also need the insight and confidence to bow out gracefully.

### Put the Responsibility for Change on Others

You can't change the behavior of other people: except for the youngest children, they must do it themselves. What you *can* do is provide others with four things:

- reasons why they might want to change
- instruction in how to change
- an environment supportive of change
- positive or negative consequences, depending on their response

Think of your goal as empowering them to change. The rest is up to them.

### Give Others Enough Time to Change

The impact you want often doesn't show as quickly as you would like. There may be years of old behavior to overcome. No wonder it can take months, or even years, for your words to sink in and affect another person's value system. People also have to escape the opposing influences in their lives before they are free to change their behavior. Until those negative reinforcers disappear, progress is unlikely. Whatever the reason for the delay, you may have to be patient and let time do its job.

Don't be surprised if behavior gets worse before it gets better. Whenever you confront another person, the first reaction to expect is a defensive one. This often causes the objectionable behavior to intensify. Sometimes the escalation is so great that you are forced to back down. Other times, you just need to ease up for a while until the initial feeling of threat dissipates.

This suggests potential value in temporarily disengaging from those who do not appear to respond to your efforts. At these times you aren't necessarily cutting your losses, but simply giving the pot a chance to boil. If nothing happens, you can come back to try again or you can accept defeat gracefully. But chances are that lessening the pressure will give others the freedom they need to change their behavior.

## Distance Yourself Mentally and Physically

At times you will simply have to give up and cut your losses. You are most likely to have to do this if the other person is one of the following:

*Manipulative:* The manipulator exploits your emotional vulnerability in order to meet his or her selfish needs. The valued employee who threatens to quit is doing this, as is the boss who says, "I don't know what I'll do if you don't help me on this one." Manipulation can become so much of a person's repertoire that even if you deal successfully with one episode of it, there is plenty more where that one came from. Some manipulators are so persistent and so effective at their craft that you can never fully neutralize them. Avoid compulsive manipulators.

*Malicious:* The truly malicious individual gets pleasure from pain inflicted on others. This person's value system can be so alien to yours that none of the appeals that work with others will work here. Don't allow malicious people to have access to you. It is especially important that both they and manipulators not learn of your vulnerabilities. Protect yourself from victimization.

*Hateful:* Some people have developed a hatred for specific groups of people, institutions, practices, or for the world in general. Unless you have the time, the motivation, and the ability to turn such people around, their anger will defeat you. In "The Caring Friend" Charlene was no match for Silvia's hatred of administrators.

*Holding conflicting values:* Here is another possible explanation for the standoff between Charlene and Silvia. Charlene respects authority, while Silvia feels it should be challenged. Neither of them is prepared to give up her outlook for the other.

*Of limited intellect:* The success of our Ten Commandments depends on your ability to provide others with compelling reasons to change their behavior. Occasionally, you may have to deal with people who simply cannot comprehend the logic of your argument.

---

*Mentally Ill:* It has been estimated that as many as twenty percent of the people you encounter daily have some form of diagnosable mental disturbance. Even a professional may have difficulty accomplishing what you hope to convince such people to do.

*Addicted:* A person who is addicted to drugs or anything else may not respond to help offered by a well-meaning nonprofessional. Give responsibility for this person to someone trained in addiction treatment.

*Low in self-esteem:* Low self-esteem is at the root of many forms of aggressive behavior. For example, the boss who bullies subordinates may simply be reflecting personal insecurities. A deficient self-concept is one of the most stubborn problems a person can have, and may present too high a hurdle for the person to clear.

*Blind to self:* "Who me?" "I did *not.*" "That's *your* opinion." These are typical phrases uttered by people who won't take a hard look at themselves. When others can't or refuse to recognize the role they play in a relationship, a major barrier has been thrown up. Even more hopeless is when they refuse to accept responsibility for their role.

## Get Help

Sometimes you must disengage from a difficult person to protect yourself from anxiety or abuse. Other times, you have to throw in the towel because you realize that more damage than good will result from persisting. Whatever your reason for backing down, this doesn't have to be the end of attempts to modify the other person's behavior. It may be the time to call in reinforcements. Perhaps a psychologist, psychiatrist, or support group can accomplish what you couldn't. A friend or family member may be able to assist. Someone else in the organization—a higher-up or a peer—might make a more appropriate intervention than you did. Don't be too proud to ask for help or let a new person take over.

### Give Yourself Credit for What You Accomplished

Don't underestimate the impact you've had. Even if the person you're dealing with hasn't shown a single sign of progress, your past efforts are likely to keep working. Over the years, Charlene made points that Silvia will recall from time to time. For example, the next time a Master Teacher is designated in the school district, Silvia may for the fleetest of moments think, "Maybe I should have listened to Charlene."

### The Essence of the Tenth Commandment

- Put the responsibility for change on others.
- Give others enough time to change.
- Distance yourself mentally and physically.

- Get help.
- Give yourself credit for what you accomplished.

---

*"Give us serenity to accept what cannot be changed, courage to change what should be changed, and wisdom to distinguish the one from the other."*

REINHOLD NIEBUHR

# II

# Advisories for Getting the Best

**If you've read** the Ten Commandments of Change over the last few days, you may already have noticed yourself behaving differently with other people. Thinking back to moments when you convinced people to work toward your goals, you should be able to spot promising examples of the Commandments in action.

In this part of the book we show you more of how to put the Commandments into practice through a series of individual advisories. We've identified forty-four different challenging people you are likely to encounter on your job, each with his or her own distinctive behaviors. For each person, we tell you what instinctive reactions to avoid and what to do and say to get the cooperation you need. In all cases, our advice grows from one or more of the Commandments.

Start by reading the description of these challenging characters. Each advisory begins with a cluster of behaviors that identifies a person you may run into. If someone giving you difficulty matches two or more of the behaviors attributed to this person, read on. The person may not exhibit all the bothersome traits—we hope not, for your sake—but you'll find good tips on how to respond.

We have divided character types by their most common roles as boss, employee, coworker, and customer. For example, the Shirker is familiar to anyone who has supervised unmotivated employees. These categories do not have strict boundaries, however. Not every Short Fuse you encounter will be a subordinate; you may even find good advice on dealing with your boss in the employee category.

When you come up against any of these trying individuals, resolve not to react dysfunctionally. The "Avoid" section lists three to six unproductive responses to reject as you deal with the person described. These represent the typical knee-jerk, emotional, or unthinking reactions that don't bring about long-lasting change—or they change the situation for the worse.

Finally, the "What to Say to Get What You Want" section recommends between four and nine strong responses, both behavioral and verbal. They all stem directly from the Ten Commandments of Change. Even so, they may not all be equally appropriate in your situation, so choose the actions that you believe will work best for you. Many of these responses include example scripts to give you ideas of exactly what to say in your situation.

### Tips on Applying the Advisories

- Become familiar with all the Advisories, even those that don't pertain to you right now. Sooner or later, as your career progresses, you'll meet all these people. Prepare for the problem before it arises.

- Difficult people can fit into more than one of the forty-four types. For example, a Turbo-powered boss may also be a Perfectionist. Check all the relevent advisories for help.

- Don't be fooled by deceptive stereotypes. Sometimes past experience or cultural imprinting blinds us to problem behaviors that seem "out of character" for a particular person. Bullies, Wimps, and the other forty-two types can be men or women, young or old. (We've alternated using *he* and *she* in the Advisories.)

- For each "What to Say" prescription, we cross-reference one or two Commandments of Change. Review those chapters to reinforce the thinking behind the advisories.

- In dealing with any difficult person, determine whether you are looking for a short-term remedy to an immediate problem or a long-term strategy that will set the person on the right track. Several of our "What to Say" ideas will put out a blaze; others aim at ongoing fire prevention. Which is your goal?

- An effective long-term career strategy is to give a copy of this book to the challenging people in your life. Ask them to note behavior in the advisories that characterizes you, and promise to do the same for them. Schedule a meeting to exchange feedback. This will make it easier for you to show them how they trouble you, and it may open your eyes to ways in which you make it difficult for them to perform well. Be prepared to listen!

- Our advice assumes that you're dealing with a rational and psychologically functional person. Statistics on mental health suggest that as much as twenty percent of the time this assumption is wrong. In such cases, the person's behavior is unlikely to change without professional intervention.

- Sometimes the people in these advisories will appear on the personal side of your life. For instance, an overcommitted friend may promise to make a date for lunch but leave you dangling; this is classic Can-Do behavior. You can use these advisories successfully outside of work; just alter your language appropriately.

# Boss Advisories

*When you respond to troubling behavior from above, act according to the reality of your relationship with your boss. Only you know how assertively you can speak to your boss. You may be able to confront him or her even more directly than these twelve advisories suggest, or you might be dismissed immediately if you followed these prescriptions.*

*Bosses are among the most difficult people in the world to change. They probably got where they are by behaving the same way they do now. Sometimes you simply have to bite the bullet, limiting your expectations for change. The Tenth Commandment—"Cut your losses with remorse, not guilt"—may apply to bosses more frequently than to employees, coworkers, and customers combined. Indeed, when the other nine commandments won't work, the only realistic solution may be to find a more satisfactory job.*

# The Puzzle

## "I shouldn't have to tell you what I expect."

- Rarely gives clear instructions.
- Provides infrequent, vague, or unclear performance evaluations.
- Sets few standards by which you can assess your performance.
- States goals in abstract terms. They are rarely quantitative or definite and almost never written down.
- Sends conflicting signals.
- Withholds information you need to do your job.

### Avoid

✗ Second guessing what the boss expects of you.

✗ Asking your coworkers what they think the boss wants you to do.

✗ Continually nagging: "Please tell me what you want me to do."

✗ Telling the boss outright, "I don't know what you expect of me," or otherwise criticizing him for giving you insufficient or inconsistent information or being difficult to work for.

✗ Bypassing the chain of command to see if his boss can give you guidance.

✗ Publicly complaining or blaming the boss.

✗ Assuming that the boss's expectations will become clearer without you taking some action.

## What to Say to Get What You Want

✔ Find out if your boss is a Puzzle to other people as well. Ask one or two coworkers, "I wish I had clearer directions from the boss: do you ever feel that way?" If they have no such difficulty, the problem may be that you haven't listened well or used common sense to read the given clues.   (2)

✔ Ask yourself, "Why isn't the boss more clear with me?" Carefully analyze his strengths, fears, concerns, and needs.   (6)

✔ Determine the major benefit the boss would derive by giving you clearer instructions. Is it more income? Reduced expenses? Better customer service? Find the right button and push it.  (8)

✔ Schedule a meeting with your boss. Lead off with, "I'm concerned that I may not be meeting the goals you have for my work." (3)

✔ Focus on the consequences of your limited access to information. "Because I'm not sure where you see the organization heading, I can't write the concluding section of my midyear report in the way that best serves your needs."  (8)

✔ Listen to your boss's response to understand his reasons for not being clear and to uncover clues about what might encourage more communication.  (2, 6)

✔ Know when to stop. Don't push beyond the flash point of impatience. "I understand your inability to be as specific as I'd like. I'll write the report with the information I have. Let me know if it fails to hit the mark."  (10)

# The Bully

## "Just do it, or find another line of work!"

- Orders rather than requests, speaks rather than listens.
- Manages through intimidation and insists on her way.
- Treats you as a child.
- Rarely asks for your ideas or suggestions.
- May show more concern for equipment and materials than for you.
- May be hostile and aggressive, pushing your buttons and engaging in emotional blackmail.

### Avoid

✗ Feeling sorry for yourself and your coworkers. Things won't get any better so long as you put your energy into self-pity.

✘ Cowering or hiding. The Bully will be emboldened by your fear.

✘ Becoming discouraged and letting your performance suffer.

✘ Getting back at the Bully through sabotage, foot-dragging, or malicious compliance; you and your career will be the ultimate losers.

✘ Enlisting a number of your colleagues to call on the boss en masse. Your "strength in numbers" will be seen as a threat, triggering the Bully to come down even harder.

✘ Bullies have an overwhelming need to win and to stay on top. Never give a powerful Bully reason to believe that you are out to beat her. She will crush you.

## What to Say to Get What You Want

✔ Study whom your boss bullies. If it's everyone, there may be little you can do. If it's just you and a few others, look for common elements in your behavior or performance for clues on how to leave this select group.   (2, 6)

✔ Recognize that you are not causing the behavior; don't look for blame in yourself. There is no excuse for being a Bully.   (10)

✔ Answer these questions as objectively and as dispassionately as possible: "What does the boss gain from being a Bully? Does her home or work environment help explain it?

What role is played by the Bully's relationship with superiors? How does she feel about her career? Is she self-confident?" Your answers will give you ideas about potential strategies. Even if you can't take action, it will help your sanity to understand what's going on.   (6, 8)

✔ Bullies want to win. If you discuss problems with the Bully, indicate how such behavior is endangering her success. Without challenging, threatening, moralizing, or judging, talk about how the behavior is lowering morale and productivity. "I find it difficult to excel under circumstances where I am pressured by more than my work; where I am unable to predict moods, and where I feel I'm not trusted. As a result, the work of my unit declines."   (1, 3)

✔ Come in with facts, numbers, and documentation. "In our most recent quality audit, my department scored only 82%. These findings released by the quality team [hold them in your hand] attest to the difficult circumstances the team felt we faced."   (2, 8)

✔ Make it in the Bully's self-interest to change. "I have plans for turning things around immediately. One of these involves a suggestion for our relationship that will empower my unit to yield the results we both know are possible. With your permission I'd like to present it."   (4, 8)

---

# The Turbo

## *"Cancel your weekend plans!"*

- Sets unreasonably high expectations for your work.
- Appears not to recognize that you have a home life.
- May give you a new assignment late Friday afternoon, expecting results Monday morning.
- Will commit to extra work for your unit without checking on your ability to meet the deadline he has promised.
- Expects you to drop whatever you're doing to respond to his needs.
- Drives himself unmercifully, and expects the same of you.

### Avoid

✗ Transferring the excessive work onto the backs of your coworkers or subordinates. You'll earn the label of "Turbo" from them.

✗ Complaining about your boss to your coworkers or to others. Chances are excellent that gripe will get back to the boss.

✗ Assuming that the work assigned to you is all busywork or that you are being punished for something. Your assignments are important to the Turbo; very few bosses use workload as punishment. Assume that the work is important, but that something has to be changed about its delegation.

## What to Say to Get What You Want

✔ Ask yourself if the boss "turbos" more with you than with anyone else. If the answer is yes, the boss may see you as a deficient performer in need of prodding.   (2, 5)

✔ Consider your assignments in context. Look at the long haul and the big picture. Do you see your boss as a Turbo simply because of a major project this weekend, or is this indeed a trend over the last six months?   (6)

✔ Seek to understand why your boss is dumping so much work on you. Are there extraordinary pressures on him in the organization? Are there urgent priorities that must be satisfied? Is there reason to expect the pressure to lessen when these priorities pass?   (2, 6)

✔ Before you confront the Turbo, ask yourself: "How can I help my boss in this interaction?

What can I do for him? What can I say that will make the boss feel better about me and about the office?" (6, 8)

✔ When you talk to your boss, don't complain, but show the impact of added work on your ability to accomplish other tasks. "Yes, boss; of course I can have this done for you by tomorrow afternoon. Of course, something else will suffer since I had planned to give two other office priorities my attention today and tomorrow." (1, 3)

✔ The Turbo has little patience with complaints or excuses; the Turbo wants solutions. "From my perspective, the original priorities are the most urgent, but if you'd like me to postpone them in order to tackle the new assignment, I will do so. Alternatively, we could get me some help for the next two days, so I can accomplish all three of them." (3, 4)

# The Showboat

## *"I led the way!"*

- Enjoys being in the limelight and receiving accolades.
- Takes credit for the success of subordinates; perhaps rose in the organization as a result of their accomplishments.
- Takes steps to get top billing whenever possible; is never satisfied to be a bit player.
- Limits your opportunity to be visible, keeping your name off reports and out of high-level staff meetings.
- Disassociates herself from high-risk projects unless they begin to pay off. Blames failure on subordinates or on bad luck. Is usually too clever to be anywhere in sight of the boss when events turn sour.

### Avoid

✗ Letting your career stagnate at the hands of a Showboat.

✗ Getting into a competitive battle with a glory-grabbing superior. The Showboat has more political savvy than you do, and will invariably win.

✗ Trying to counter the Showboat's headlining by revealing the true heroes behind victories. If you're discovered, you will have a threatened and angry boss on your hands. Even if she never finds out, someone else is bound to. You can't win with a reputation for sabotaging someone else's career.

✗ Complaining to the Showboat's superiors.

✗ Allowing any aspect of your behavior to be seen as career-threatening by the Showboat.

## What to Say to Get What You Want

✔ Find out if others see the boss as a Showboat. If most coworkers disagree with you on this, it may be that you either are jealous of your boss's success or have an unrealistic view of your value compared to hers.   (2)

✔ Showboats are highly concerned about their images and very sensitive to criticism. Therefore, you may choose not to address the issue directly. The best strategy may be to continue to help your boss look good, while exerting the same energy on garnering equal kudos for yourself.   (4, 8)

✔ Seek every opportunity to make your work more visible in the organization. Succeed on big jobs; gain authorship of widely disseminated reports; get your name in the company newsletter; make presentations to senior staff. (1, 10)

✔ Offer to tag along to staff meetings to buttress your boss's position with whatever unique data you might possess. This way you can increase her effectiveness and your visibility at the same time. "I'd be happy to assist you in preparing for and even in delivering the presentation you need to make at next week's staff meeting." (1, 4)

✔ Look for opportunities in the organization to network: with your peers, with other managers at your boss's level, and with customers or other powerful groups. But take special care not to be perceived as behaving inappropriately or being a glory-grabber. (3, 6)

✔ If you choose to confront the Showboat directly, deal with concrete examples: "I'm concerned that the value of my work is not always matched by the amount of exposure it receives. My contribution to the annual report represented the majority of the final result. Yet my name was not on it when presented to senior staff. While it was rewarding to work on that project, it was discouraging not to receive due credit. Can you help me understand what I can do to keep this from happening again?" (1, 3)

# The Ostrich

*"I can't ask them to do that; they'll be all over me."*

- Avoids confrontation at all costs. Sees conflict as destructive.

- Responds to disagreements among subordinates by ignoring them, by asking people not to fight, or by smoothing over differences. Won't dig to the root of the disagreement.

- Doesn't want to hear bad news. In fact, may punish the bearer of bad tidings.

- For the sake of being liked, will accept mediocrity, tolerate unacceptable behavior, and fail to address situations where a decisive response might generate controversy.

- Ignores the signs of poor performance whenever employee behavior is the cause. Absenteeism may rise, productivity may decline, quality may decay, and the turnover rate may soar, but the Ostrich doesn't admit there's a problem.

- The Ostrich's favorite bumper stickers are "Live and Let Live" and "If It Ain't Broke, Don't Fix It."
- Fails to criticize employees—even those who deserve it.

## Avoid

✗ Challenging the Ostrich. He is easily threatened.

✗ Bringing unsolved problems to the Ostrich's attention without a palatable remedy.

✗ Frightening the Ostrich. Confrontation with irrefutable evidence is likely to force the Ostrich to bury his head in the sand even more than it is right now.

✗ Becoming an Ostrich yourself.

✗ Prefacing disagreement with an Ostrich with the phrase, "I disagree." Instead, raise "what if . . . " questions.

✗ Defining problems as such. Suggest, instead, that there is simply another way of looking at something. Don't point out how your views differ from those of the Ostrich, or why a conflict exists. Rather show other views of the situation.

## What to Say to Get What You Want

✔ Find out who agrees with you that the boss is an Ostrich. Perhaps it's only those subordinates who make unreasonable requests, are militantly confrontational, or have abrasive styles. You're not one of these, are you?   (2, 5)

✔ Study the Ostrich in order to understand the cause of his behavior. Is it a personality tendency? A reflection of his home life? Attributable to his relations with superiors? Do subordinates, and you in particular, pose a threat to the Ostrich?   (6)

✔ See that your disagreements with others get resolved before they get to your boss.   (5)

✔ Emphasize the positive to the Ostrich before you get to the problems that need to be addressed. The Ostrich may even benefit from some positive reinforcement, but be careful not to be an obvious boot-licker. "Boss, we have a wonderful opportunity to improve quality in the marketing department. For a long time, as you know, David and Maurita have not seen eye-to-eye on the relative merit of print versus electronic advertising. While they haven't resolved their disparate views, we have gained a great deal from the research they did. We now have the potential for a marketing plan that will be more data-driven than that of our competitors."   (7, 8)

✔ Offer solutions to the Ostrich. "I suggest a meeting where we reconcile Maurita's and David's philosophies and emerge with a marketing strategy that will propel us into the future."   (4, 8)

✔ Get the Ostrich out of situations he can't handle. Your lifesaving is not likely to go unnoticed by the boss or by superiors. "I'll be happy to chair the meeting with your guidance and keep you fully informed." (7, 8)

✔ Each day ask yourself, "What solutions [not problems] can I present to my boss today?"   (8)

✔ When the Ostrich panics, back down. Come back later with a more agreeable strategy. (7, 10)

# The Dumper

*"I'm turning all my calls over to you this week so I can reorganize my files."*

- Delegates *too much*—a rare quality in managers.
- Doesn't work nearly as hard as her employees.
- Has a spotless office and a clean desk because everyone else is doing all the work.
- Stays busy with easy tasks and fun jobs. The Dumper may take two days to create an elegant employee vacation calendar for next year; her client meetings may consume two-hour lunches and mornings on the golf course; travel is sometimes an "urgent" priority.

- Sees time management as delegating knotty problems and challenging tasks to everybody else. However, the authority you need to handle such responsibilities may not be part of the deal.
- Usually does not have a demanding boss.

## Avoid

✗ Accusing the Dumper of giving you all of her work.

✗ Retaliating through sabotage, backbiting, or political maneuvering. Don't complain to the Dumper's boss that she is not doing a fair share of the work.

✗ The Dumper's survival as a Dumper shows that she is powerful enough to leave attackers in the dust. Don't be foolish enough to believe that the nobility of your cause will carry it to victory.

✗ Dumping on your subordinates as a way of cleaning up your desk.

## What to Say to Get What You Want

✔ Do an objective analysis of the Dumper's behavior. Does the boss delegate to everyone equally, or do you get more than your share? What does this distribution suggest to you? Is the "dumping" on you perhaps a positive sign of her trust in you?   (2, 5)

✔ The most sensible strategy may be simply to work around the Dumper. Don't confront the behavior: the Dumper is likely to deny it, and may become angry. Work at becoming more efficient so that you can handle all the work the Dumper is going to throw your way.   (6, 10)

✔ The best time to negotiate responsibilities is when the Dumper is actually putting projects on your desk. Do it in a nonthreatening way. Don't challenge the boss's authority and don't accuse her of dumping on you; instead, ask questions about what you can count on her to contribute. "In order for me to serve you well on this assignment, I need to know now where our respective responsibilities begin and end. Without such clarity, I may expect something from you that is not realistic, and the project could fail as a result. For example, I have never been able to convince the comptroller to give priority to the financial analyses required by these kinds of projects. May I count on you, and even remind you if necessary, to use your authority?"   (1, 3)

✔ Consider that the short-term frustration of working for a Dumper may be acting to your long-term benefit. The more of the Dumper's responsibility that is given to you, the more opportunity you have to look good in the organization.   (10)

# The Pet Owner

*"Why can't I count on you people the way I can count on Marlene?"*

- Responds to employees according to how much he likes them.

- Gives pets the best assignments at the expense of others. They also receive more benefits than those who haven't managed to get on the pet list.

- Has favorites who flatter, don't rock the boat, bring good news, like his ideas, or come from the "right" side of the tracks.

- Treats nonfavorites more or less decently, but with more detachment, perhaps a higher degree of professionalism, and less personal investment. For example, the Pet Owner will spend hours teaching a favored employee while others are lucky to get the time of day.

- Frequently holds up the work of pets as an example.

   *N.B.* Pet ownership becomes more seriously complicated and more organizationally destructive whenever the relationship is sexually or racially motivated.

## Avoid

✗ Becoming angry at people who have been selected as pets. Most employees are equally interested in getting in the boss's good graces. Furthermore, they have not created the situation—the boss has.

✗ Allowing your concern over the Pet Owner's behavior to affect your performance. Don't whine or pout.

✗ Being dumb enough to think that the Pet Owner's boss will thank you for bringing this situation to his or her attention.

✗ Accusing the Pet Owner of being one. Pet Owners are convinced that they respond to employees fairly. When they do admit to preferential treatment, they base it on the performance they perceive: "I give back to those employees who give to the organization and to me."

## What to Say to Get What You Want

✔ Ask yourself if the boss is sending you an important message. Examine your role in your relationship with the Pet Owner. Do you refuse to play office politics out of a sense of moral indignation? If so, you should seriously consider going to work for yourself—the only chance you may have to escape such games.   (2)

✔ Consider the possibility that the Pet Owner's reaction to you may have to do with the quality of your performance in comparison with others'. Do you really give what your boss is looking for just as well as the so-called pets? If you were accused of being a top performer, would there be enough evidence to convict you?   (5)

✔ Take a close look at the favored treatment. Is the favoritism being shown in tangible or in subtle ways? For example, if you believe coworkers are getting extra pay or benefits, you may be staring a discrimination case in the face. Consider contacting your local affirmative action or EEOC office.   (1)

✔ You may have to look elsewhere in the organization for the mentorship you'll need to move ahead. Consider another job.   (10)

✔ Seek out opportunities to be involved in projects likely to lead to publicized success and high visibility. Become known outside of your department as a rising star.   (10)

✔ Come up with at least three good answers to this question: "What can I do to cause my boss to feel the same way about me that he seems to feel about others?"   (4, 8)

✔ Ask the boss: "What would enable me to become an even more valued employee to you? Please tell me three things I can do more of and three things I can do less of that would enhance my service to you." (5, 6)

✔ Declare your intention to work hard for your boss. "I want to improve my performance in this department and to gain more recognition from you as one of your indispensable employees. I want to look good for both of us." (3, 8)

# The Chicken

## *"My boss will never go for that."*

- Fears going to bat for you and your colleagues. Chickens won't risk their relationships with their bosses to go out on a limb for you.

- Doesn't have enough influence over superiors to get you what you need in order to do your job.

- Qualifies most decisions and seems very hesitant, almost timid. The Chicken is more likely to procrastinate than to make a decision.

- Censors your ideas before they get to the boss to avoid offense.

- Won't voice disagreement with superiors; waffles in front of top management even when she has definite views; buckles under to arrogant customers.

- Is intimidated by colleagues; rarely obtains the department's fair share of organizational resources or favor.

- Usually looks the other way when employees should be corrected.

## Avoid

✗ Confronting a Chicken directly. This will intimidate her even more, and may result in retaliation.

✗ Back-stabbing, name-calling, or venting your frustration publicly with coworkers.

✗ Going around the Chicken to higher-ups.

## What to Say to Get What You Want

✔ Listen closely to make the Chicken feel important. Hang on every word when she speaks.   (1, 7)

✔ Be encouraging. Whenever the Chicken expresses concern about a situation, or a fear of taking some information to top management, point out the merits of her position. "Don't give up too quickly. The boss will really be impressed with your supporting data."   (4)

✔ Whenever you hear someone call your boss a Chicken or comment on an "inferiority complex," stand up for her—or at least be silent. "That may not be a fair characterization. I'm not so sure we'd handle it any differently if we were faced with the same pressures."   (7)

✔ Retain and assert your own realistic optimism in situations where the Chicken may be afraid. "The employees will love your presentation. They've waited for a long time to learn about the reorganization. Not only will they appreciate your honesty and full disclosure, they'll also like most of the new reporting structure. Knock 'em dead!"   (5)

✔ Allay the Chicken's fears by pointing out probabilities or past experience. "I've never known anyone on the senior staff to react in that way. The worst that's ever happened is . . ."   (6)

✔ Make every effort to build the Chicken's self-esteem. "We in the department are really behind you on this, and are convinced that the direction you are taking on this year's budget negotiations is right on the mark."   (5)

✔ Ask if the Chicken would like you to represent her in situations where you know you may be able to speak for the department more forcefully. "Regarding the budget negotiations coming up next week in the company, I want you to know that I stand ready to help in any way that I can. I would be happy to create summary sheets on that research, and provide any other assistance you may need."   (8)

# The Hypocrite

---

*"You wouldn't
mind typing my
son's term paper
this afternoon,
would you?"*

---

- Asks you to do things he's unwilling to do.

- Says one thing to your face and does another behind your back. The Hypocrite may condemn the very behavior that characterizes his leadership performance.

- Maintains two sets of rules, one for employees and one for the boss. For example, the Hypocrite expects you to perform beyond the call of duty and to save money. But while you're counting your paper clips, switching to cheap pens, and writing on both sides of the sheet, he's ordering the finest wines on his cross-country business jaunts.

---

- Criticizes you for treating your subordinates in the same way he treats you and your colleagues.

- Sends you off to learn leadership skills, but won't support you when you attempt to practice them. For example, you return from a seminar on employee motivation with an idea for an employee recognition program; the Hypocrite refuses to invest in it.

- Behaves inconsistently, appearing to operate from one organizational vision today and a completely different one tomorrow.

## Avoid

✗ Allowing your moral indignation to get the best of you.

✗ Getting so upset at the Hypocrite that you forget common sense. In other words, don't drop down into your stomach to complain and suffer. Stay in your head to devise a way to win.

✗ Accusing the Hypocrite of being one. No one engaged in the business of hypocrisy ever hung out a shingle.

✗ Looking for a way to expose the problem. The Hypocrite's boss is probably aware of the Hypocrite's behavior and has chosen not to act. This neglect should say something to you about the success of exposure.

## What to Say to Get What You Want

✔ Check the perceptions of your coworkers. Do they also see the boss as a Hypocrite, or are you being too critical?   (2)

✔ If you choose to confront the Hypocrite, don't ascribe intent, don't accuse, don't complain that he's being unfair. Instead, focus on the gap between what the Hypocrite believes and what others perceive. "The recent request to have us cut back on departmental expenses has hit a sour note within the department. While we all see the need to reduce expenses, and are willing to make the necessary sacrifices—including buying our own pens to write with—we don't see upper management undergoing the same belt-tightening. The recent management retreat in the Bahamas is a good example of that. No matter how important it may have been, it created enormous dissension."   (3, 4)

✔ Without condoning the Hypocrite's behavior, you can point out that the behavior is not the problem; the problem is the way the behavior is perceived. Then, the remedies you suggest to eliminate the perception can in fact be strategies designed to curb the actual hypocrisy. "There may be justifications, but all we can respond to is what is in plain view. Please help to eliminate the perception around here that management is unwilling to bear its share of the cost-cutting burden."   (7, 8)

✔ Offer a recommendation for dealing with perceived hypocrisy. "If we are going to get the rank and file to take cost-cutting seriously, we have to set a more convincing example for them. Let me suggest that . . ." (1, 3)

✔ You may ultimately have to cut your losses and accept that this behavior is a part of your boss. If anything is going to be done, the action may have to come from above. (10)

# The Deaf Ear

*"I don't have time right now; please make an appointment."*

- Rarely has time to listen to employees' problems.

- Cares little about the opinions of others.

- Is not approachable or easily accessible.

- Believes a meeting is really a forum for the dissemination of the boss's ideas. When the Deaf Ear asks for questions, you'd better not have any.

- Cuts off your ideas in mid-sentence with a response that bears no necessary connection to your statement. The Deaf Ear's comments often appear to come out of a totally different discussion.

- Sees most complaints as unjustified.

- Is often heard to say, "We tried that before," or, "That won't work."
- Accuses others of being poor listeners.

## Avoid

✗ Talking louder or faster; it won't help.

✗ Accusing the Deaf Ear of being a poor listener.

✗ Assuming that the Deaf Ear is cold, insensitive, or mean-spirited. She may be all of these, she may be none of these. All you know is that the Deaf Ear is not listening to you. It is that behavior you wish to change, not the underlying attitude.

✗ Seeking solace on the shoulders of others. Don't look for people to complain to; you need to solve this problem with your boss.

✗ Excessively prefacing your messages: "You're probably busy right now, but . . . " Especially don't apologize for news: "I'm sorry to be the one to tell you . . . "

✗ Phrasing statements as questions, or putting tag lines on the ends of your ideas: "This is a good way to look at it—*don't you think*?"

## What to Say to Get What You Want

✔ Carefully consider what in your communication style may turn off your boss's ears. Is your message focused? Do you beat around the bush? One reason why your boss may not be listening to you is that you may not be a "listenable" employee. Before you open your mouth, ask yourself, "How can I send this message so it will get through?" (2, 5)

✔ Send messages to your boss at the time, in the place, and in the format that experience has told you are best. (6)

✔ In your communications, focus on the Deaf Ear's self-interest. Before speaking to your boss ask yourself what hot buttons you can push. "I have an idea for getting a forty percent return on a small investment in overtime in my department." (8)

✔ End your sentences with exclamation points, not question marks. Make your voice trail up at the end of your statements. (5, 6)

✔ Monitor your nonverbal messages. Maintain eye contact and an erect posture. Avoid monotones or sing-song variations in your voice. Don't fiddle with anything. (5)

✔ Get your facts straight before you speak. Know your exact purpose in speaking. Organize your presentation in the most compelling fashion. "You don't have to worry about cost overruns on the project any longer. With your approval today, we can head off $97,000 in unnecessary expenditures." (3, 5)

✔ Speak clearly and distinctly. Get to the bottom line quickly. Use "you," not "I." "Your report to higher-ups will be more convincing if you include this information." (8)

✔ Give evidence for your assertions. Support complicated briefings with outlines and written material. "This is what it will take: (1) switching to ACME, Inc. for spare parts delivery, for a $29,000 savings, (2) starting the engine assembly three weeks sooner by using the closed west wing of the southside plant, for a $45,000 savings, and (3) cannibalizing a used rotor for our rotor assembly, for a savings of $23,000." (5, 6)

# The Withholder

## *"Don't ask why; just do it."*

- Won't delegate authority.
- Manages very close to the vest. Feels that the best decisions are decisions that he makes; is reluctant to share the decision-making process. Announces plans without asking for feedback.
- Rarely gives you enough information to do your job, even though he may have that information at hand.
- Gives little feedback on the quality of your effort; does not offer adequate praise or criticism.
- Seems to filter information from superiors. Believes that the only information you deserve is what you need to do your job, which turns out to be a small fraction of what will empower you to make your greatest contribution to the organization.
- May be clear in telling you *what* to do but rarely tells you *why*. Is more likely to tell you

*how* to do something than to allow you to use your own imagination.

## Avoid

✗ Trying to get information from your boss's boss. That action will return to haunt you.

✗ Second guessing what the boss wants—unless you're a certified mind-reader.

✗ Making assumptions about what the boss thinks of the quality of your work. Find out.

✗ Allowing the lack of needed information to cause you to fail.

✗ Accepting assignments without the authority that you'll need to carry them out.

## What to Say to Get What You Want

✔ Ask yourself whether all employees complain about being kept in the dark by your boss. If you are one of the few who complain, you are likely to be at least partially responsible for the boss's reluctance to be more forthcoming. What might you have done to lose his trust? What other sources of information do people use?   (2, 5)

✔ When a job is delegated to you, make certain you understand it well enough to anticipate the authority, the resources, the information, and the time you need to complete it. Ask the boss for each of these. "Before I start this project, I'll need to know exactly what supervisory authority you expect me to exert, the discretion I have to order supplies as needed, the firmness of the deadline we've been given by the contractor, and your availability to help me with snags." (1, 3)

✔ Ask the boss for feedback on how well you're doing your job. The best way is to ask for three lists: (1) what you should be doing more of, (2) what you should be doing less of, and (3) what you should keep the same. You'll be even more likely to get a response if you relate it to a specific assignment rather than to your overall performance. "Boss, sometimes I think I did a good job for you and other times I'm less certain. With regard to the report I gave you yesterday, I would like to ask you specifically what would you have liked to have seen more of in that report, what should I have done less of, and what did you really like? In other words, how can I improve the next report I turn in?" (3, 4)

✔ Suggest specific ways in which the Withholder will gain from consulting subordinates in decision making. "Many of the headaches you have with that job can be eliminated. For example, Jack and Lynn would like to speak with you about their ideas for reducing customer complaints by at least 50%." (4, 8)

✔ Learn the organizational rationale for new assignments. "May I ask where you see this project fitting into our quality improvement program? Before I begin it, I want to make certain my work makes the maximum contribution to the bottom line." (3, 5)

# The Perfectionist

## *"It's not right until I say it is!"*

- Insists you do the job her way—the "right" way.

- Thinks results are never good enough. The Perfectionist has higher standards than anyone is capable of achieving, but rarely makes those standards clear at the outset.

- Catches people in mistakes, rarely victory.

- Qualifies what little praise she gives: "Thanks for your effort. I'm sure you'll be able to do an even better job next time."

- Overreacts to minor mistakes. The Perfectionist expects the best from everyone, gets upset with anything less. Little errors become major catastrophes.

- Doesn't understand the difference between insisting upon quality and expecting perfection. Quality is doing the right thing right the first time as often as conditions allow; perfection is doing the right thing the boss's way every time.

## Avoid

✗ Manifesting the same behavior with your subordinates.

✗ Seeing your inability to satisfy the Perfectionist as a flaw in your performance or a shortcoming in your value as an employee (or worse yet, as a person). You may not be perfect, but it doesn't mean you're a poor performer.

✗ Mistakenly condemning every boss who insists on high quality as a Perfectionist.

✗ Confusing quality with perfection. The highest quality is a standard that all companies should strive for. Conversely, perfection never occurs, and is therefore a mirage that frustrates our attempts to reach it. Even if we could achieve perfection, the enormous incremental cost of creating it could not possibly be worth the outcome.

## What to Say to Get What You Want

✔ Look around at your colleagues. Is their work acceptable to the suspected Perfectionist? If it is, your boss may not be the problem. Are you willing to go the extra mile to achieve quality? (2, 5)

---

✔ Listen carefully to everything the Perfectionist says. Whenever you can, repeat demands; this gives her an opportunity to hear how unreasonable they are. "You're saying even though your boss asked me to handle the customer the way I did, that I'm to call the customer back and renege on my promise?" (2, 4)

✔ Ask for specific reasons why the way you're doing something will not meet the Perfectionist's goals. Do so in a nonthreatening, nonaggressive manner. Be prepared for the possibility that the explanation *will* satisfy you. "I aimed for a report consistent with the understanding I had when I left your office. Please point out to me why my assumptions were wrong so that next month I might give you what you need the first time." (2, 5)

✔ Before undertaking any task assigned to you by a Perfectionist, get a very clear statement of expectations. Be certain the direction you take will satisfy her. "Before I implement the new procedure, I want to make sure we're on the same wavelength. These are the three steps I'll take and the results I'll look for. . . . Am I missing anything?" (3)

# Employee Advisories

*Your success in motivating employees will largely depend on the relationship you maintain with your own boss. If he or she backs up your actions, you should be empowered to do everything we suggest here and more. Without your boss's support, your ability to respond to undesirable subordinate behavior is severely compromised.*

*Of the various powers one may utilize in dealing with subordinates, the most important is the ability to mete out rewards and punishments. If employees see you as the source of tangible benefits, such as pay raises, and if you have the ability to hire and fire, your position is much stronger. Remember that your employees are individuals; some respond to the stick, and some to the carrot. A good supervisor can motivate both ways.*

# The Wimp

> *"Would it be all right for me to move ahead with this?"*

- Is nonassertive, even with subordinates.
- Checks with you unnecessarily for authorization to begin projects, for approval of work to date, and for agreement to continue.
- Avoids high-risk, high-gain actions.
- Says little in meetings. When the Wimp does speak, it sounds more like a question than a statement.
- Excessively qualifies, prefaces, and apologizes for ideas: "Boss, I realize you're busy, and there probably isn't money in the budget, and you may not like the idea anyway, but . . ."
- Tends to downplay or negate praise: "No, I could have done a lot better than that."

## Avoid

✗ Enabling the Wimp by agreeing with, or even listening to, any inappropriately self-deprecating statements.

✗ Condemning the person, rather than her action, when the Wimp misses the mark.

✗ Giving assignments that require interaction with critical people, calling for skills beyond those the Wimp now possesses.

✗ Accusing the Wimp of being insecure. She already knows.

## What to Say to Get What You Want

✔ Examine your interaction with the Wimp for possible ways you contribute to her problem. For example, are you an intimidating boss? (2, 5)

✔ Put the Wimp in situations where her efforts are most likely to succeed and lead to visible results. (7)

✔ Help the Wimp to set and look forward to ambitious goals. Force her to create plans to achieve those goals. Provide coaching and counseling as she works on them. (1)

✔ Put the Wimp in a position to help someone else—perhaps training a new employee. It is very difficult to have a positive impact on others and not be uplifted yourself. (4, 7)

✔ When the Wimp comes to you for unnecessary guidance, answer questions with questions of your own. "What have you done so far? How would you handle it if you were me? If you *did* have an opinion, what would it be? How will you handle it next time?"   (3, 4)

✔ Link the Wimp with other subordinates who have high self-esteem and the success that generally accompanies such self-esteem. (4, 5)

✔ You may want to engage in self-effacing behaviors. Laugh at your mistakes, admit your failures, or share your fears and weaknesses. Show the Wimp that your imperfections have not translated into disaster, and in fact have ultimately proven to be assets. "Did I ever tell you about the first time I had to make a presentation to my boss? One of her assistants told me afterwards that they had to wipe up my sweat from the conference table with a paper towel."   (5)

✔ Get into the Wimp's shoes. Think hard about the possible benefits she can gain by becoming more assertive. Show how those benefits will result from your suggestions. "While I can't guarantee anything, you can be certain that the next time pay raises are dished out, those who have risen to higher-level challenges and who have risked for the company are going to be at a distinct advantage. I would like to see *you* having that advantage."   (3, 8)

✔ Document past successes. Force the Wimp to see exactly what she did well, and how it has benefitted the organization. "The last client you served remarked that you are the most professional, thorough, and competent they have encountered. As a result, we'll be getting their business for a long time to come. And guess who they insist be their contact?"   (6, 9)

✔ Give the Wimp a chance to talk about his or her concerns. "Please tell me what makes you feel that way."   (2)

✔ Don't belittle the Wimp's concerns. Agree that the difficulties are really there before you say how they can be overcome. "I hear you. You're right about the challenge as well as about your lack of experience with this sort of thing. But just look at how much you've accomplished in the last two years [give examples]."   (4, 7)

✔ If you uncover a fear of failing, make it clear that in your role as coach you will hold the safety net. "Not only that, I'll be here every step of the way with my full support."   (1, 7)

✔ If the Wimp does move ahead more boldly in the organization, don't just think she has finally had the sense to do something for herself. Actually, this employee has done something for you, too: convey your feelings about that. "I know that you were concerned about your ability to satisfy that client. But look at how thoroughly you have succeeded. Thank you for taking the risk, and thank you for getting in there with both hands and feet. You've made my job easier, and made me look good at the same time."   (9)

# The Griper

*"How can I soar
like an eagle when
I have to work
with turkeys?"*

- Complains about peers; often reports their
  failings as reasons for his own failures. Keeps
  track of the mistakes of coworkers.
- Often claims you're not giving him enough
  time or resources to complete projects.
- Worries about what will go wrong without
  giving equal billing to expected gains.
- Is highly critical of others' work. He enters
  their presence looking for the worst—and
  always seems to find it.
- Resists change. Can give you a dozen reasons
  why an innovation won't work. Immediately
  sees the weakness in every idea proposed by
  others.
- Often says, "I told you so."

- Brings bad news with glee.
- Harps at you about problems caused by your behavior; nitpicks at almost everything you do or say.

## Avoid

✗ Becoming angry, a natural reaction. The Griper is especially difficult for positive-thinking managers to deal with.

✗ Attributing to malice what can be explained by incompetence. Few Gripers intend to rain on other people's parades. Most of them wreak even more damage on their own lives than they do on yours. They need help.

✗ Agreeing with a Griper wholeheartedly even if you think he is right.

✗ Assuming that there is no merit to the complaint. Even Gripers bring worthy situations to your attention at times. Listen long enough every time to separate the wheat from the chaff.

✗ Letting the negative attitude of the Griper turn you into a pessimist.

## What to Say to Get What You Want

✔ Count the number of Gripers in your life. If you discover more than a handful, you may not be open to the valid concerns of others. If there are many Gripers in your organization, look for the primary cause in the actions of top management.   (2)

✔ Maintain your own realistic optimism, even in the face of the Griper's negativity.   (5)

✔ In critical decision situations, bring in the Griper *after* tentative decisions have been made. He will ensure that any disadvantages of the chosen alternative are fully explored. "Tell us what you think we've missed in this decision."   (6)

✔ State your perception of situations affirmatively but not argumentatively. "I appreciate the objectivity you bring to the project: the devil's advocate approach keeps us aware of potential negative outcomes. The problem with your focus, however, is its tone. Your voice sounds so gloomy when you identify potential hazards that others get discouraged."   (3, 4)

✔ Show your enthusiasm not just in what you say, but in how you say it. Have an upbeat look, an upbeat personality, and manage your department with an unmistakable passion. Look, act, and sound as if you believe in your goals and in your plans.   (5)

✔ Focus the Griper on the benefits of the change. "The new performance review system will eliminate an adversarial tone by making it less a judgment of you and more a chance for us to exchange feedback with each other."   (8)

✔ Give status to the Griper's resistance. Admit that the problems the Griper sees may be real but show how they are mitigated. "You're correct in describing how I've sometimes mishandled disagreement among members of our team, but that's in the past. I've learned from those mistakes and will never repeat them. Now, lets get back to what I've asked you to do." (6, 7)

✔ Force the Griper to make positive contributions before voicing criticisms. "At today's meeting I want you to play *angel's* advocate. Discipline yourself to make a positive comment before you make a critical one." (3, 4)

# The Blamer

## *"It's not my fault."*

- Blames personal failures on other people.
- Refuses to accept responsibility for poor performance.
- Is highly critical of others—much more critical of them than of herself. May also blame you, the supervisor, for problems.
- Looks for external causes for performance shortfalls, such as the difficulty of the assignment, inadequate information, not enough resources, poor cooperation, or bad luck. The Blamer is not enough of a self-critic to say, "Maybe I screwed up."
- May see herself as a victim of environment without the ability to change it.

### Avoid

✗ Becoming an enabler. Don't let the Blamer claim irrelevant external causes or dismiss her contribution to failure. Gently but firmly document the role the Blamer played in the outcome.

✗ Counterattacking a Blamer who uses you as a scapegoat. Don't become angry or defensive. Don't attack the Blamer; attack the problem.

✗ Setting the wrong example for the Blamer. When you become highly critical of others, you reinforce the very behavior you are trying to change.

## What to Say to Get What You Want

✔ Focus the Blamer on the present and future and away from the past. "The past is the past; let's bury it. In fact, for our discussion today, let's agree to refrain from talking about anything that happened prior to this discussion." (1, 4)

✔ Without accepting or denying what the Blamer is claiming, ask what she thinks it will take to improve matters. "We are both paid to get results. In this situation that means our focus needs to be on fixing the problem, not the blame. What can we do to prevent a recurrence?" (2, 3)

✔ Make sure when you delegate a project you are delegating responsibility, accountability, and resources. Make it impossible for the Blamer to claim that lack of these resources was to blame for her poor performance. Indeed, go out of your way to illustrate just how much discretion you are giving her. "With the new responsibility you are assuming, I want us to set very clear goals and agree on how those goals are going to be achieved. I need you to tell me exactly what I can do to help you perform your job and what help you are expecting from every other person in this office. It must be perfectly clear to all what their roles are and what you're counting on them to do. Finally, I won't accept excuses for failure unless I'm informed about problems the very same day they come to your attention. If you'll agree to bring them to my attention immediately, I'll either help you solve them or let you off the hook."   (1, 3)

✔ After assigning work, insist that the Blamer restate your expectations. "To avoid some of our past misunderstandings, tell me in your own words what you see yourself as accountable for on this project."
(3, 4)

✔ Listen closely to make the Blamer feel important. Don't necessarily agree, and tell her when you don't. Ultimately, you may have to assert the power of your position. "I hear what you're saying about what went wrong, and I've thought carefully about the merits of your argument. You also know how it looks to me, and why I came to the conclusion I did. You may not agree with me, but the judgment I made will have to be the one that prevails here. And I have a feeling that if the responsibility for results were yours, you might make the same decision I did."   (1, 3)

✔ Place the Blamer in situations where she will be encouraged to think more about the role she plays in relationships. Send the Blamer to a seminar on dealing with difficult people; give her the opportunity to see herself on videotape; assign her to work with assertive, no-nonsense coworkers.   (1, 4)

# The Denier

## *"Who, me?"*

- Refuses to acknowledge a problem with his performance—even in the face of compelling evidence.
- Can fight with a coworker one minute, and then vehemently deny that there's a disagreement.
- Is unrealistic about his ability to produce. May also have an inflated opinion of his personal skills.
- Is defensive when criticized.
- Seems neither to know nor to understand what effect he has in the work group.
- May disagree with you about what constitutes good performance. If not, may disagree with you about how good performance should be measured.
- May lie to you to cover up some deficiency.

### Avoid

✗ Letting the Denier get away with dishonesty. Otherwise, other employees will resent your lack of courage, and the Denier will be more emboldened.

✗ Getting into a battle of accusations. The Denier will just walk away convinced you're a jerk.

✗ Calling this person a liar even if you know his information has been fabricated. The Denier won't admit to lying.

✗ Allowing the Denier to drag you down to the same level of emotionality or mud-slinging.

✗ Permitting the Denier to procrastinate or delay meeting with you regarding performance problems. Arrange the meeting yourself at a time and place convenient for him.


## What to Say to Get What You Want

✔ Count the number of Deniers you have working for you. If you have more than your share, you may intimidate employees to the point that they are afraid to admit their errors.   (2, 5)

✔ The key to dealing with a Denier is to avoid a shouting match or discussion of "what if," and "I thought," and "you meant." To prevent this, deal with clear expectations. These need to be *written down*. "To make certain we agree on how this job is to be done, I've drafted a one page summary of my expectations. As soon as we can both agree on them, we will use them as criteria for evaluating your performance. And if you have expectations for how I can support you, please write those down and get back to me with them by tomorrow." (1, 3)

✔ Focus the Denier on needs and issues, away from emotions and demands. Confront him with data, not hearsay or speculation. "Here is the bottom line. You don't believe that the disagreement between the two stock clerks is serious or that it's any of my business. However, it is harming the performance of this team in these ways. . . . Until those performance barriers are cleared, the present situation is unacceptable. Let's talk about what it will take to clear it up." (3, 4)

✔ Make sure the Denier and all of your employees realize that your role is helping them to do their job better. Two of your main goals are representing them to upper management and getting what they need to do their jobs. "My job around here is to serve you. I'll do my best to get you what you need to succeed. And when you support the goals of our team, I'll go to bat for you with upper management." (5, 8)

✔ With the Denier you may want to lose to win. That is, you may accept what a Denier says, or at least not refute it, but then proceed to indicate what your various specific expectations are for *the future*. "It doesn't look as though you and I are ever going to be able to agree about exactly what happened.

I'm willing to call it a draw. The past doesn't interest me nearly as much as the future. Here are my specific expectations for the next time you conduct performance reviews on your staff. I've written them down for our mutual convenience. Please look them over and raise questions before you leave my office." (1, 4)

✔ When all else fails, you might urge the Denier to seek work elsewhere. "Last year we both agreed to progress toward a more productive relationship. For the reasons I just outlined, your side of the agreement has not been upheld. Let's talk about conditions of your termination that will be in the best interests of the company while giving you opportunity to find other employment." (3, 10)

# The Shirker

## *"How can you ask me to do that?"*

- Brings little commitment and excitement to work.

- Lacks ambition; may not desire to progress through the ranks of the organization or excel in the profession. Avoids situations involving increased responsibility.

- Appears to be lazy; enjoys a workday with little to do. Works slowly. Dreads busy days. Constantly complains about having too much to do, but is rarely seen doing it.

- Shows little initiative, energy, or diligence. Rarely acts unless requested or urged to do so. Does what is required, but little more. Often fails to follow through on commitments.

- Does not produce high-quality work; performs just well enough to get by.

■ Often tells more responsible employees that they work too hard, and may even discourage them from generating so much output.

## Avoid

✗ Making it easy for the Shirker to get out of responsibilities. Don't come to the rescue when the Shirker claims a job is too much. Leave the monkey on her back.

✗ Allowing the Shirker to bask in the collective praise of a hardworking staff.

✗ Accusing the Shirker of being lazy, stupid, unambitious, or malicious. You'll just give her more reason to underachieve.

✗ Complaining to the Shirker's coworkers. It's not their job to help. You'll simply look ineffectual to them.

## What to Say to Get What You Want

✔ Recruit and select the very best candidates for your team to minimize the number of Shirkers you'll have to deal with.   (1)

✔ Model the behavior you want from employees. Show enthusiasm. Show commitment. Show energy. Show follow-through.   (5)

✔ Examine this employee's behavior with respect to the other people you supervise. If this individual stands out, you probably do have a Shirker on your hands. If, however, many of the people under you show Shirker symptoms, the root of the problem is more likely in your leadership style or in the organizational culture.   (2, 5)

✔ Make your expectations for hard work clear to all your subordinates—especially the Shirker. Reinforce the fact that promotions, merit increases, and other rewards depend on fulfilling these expectations. "This year we'll be expected to do more with less. The pressure for performance is on, and I look for it to continue. If we don't produce, the organization might die; any employee who won't produce is standing in our way. Your choice is to become extraordinary or expendable. One hundred percent effort will be rewarded generously."   (1, 3)

✔ Give the Shirker specific feedback. Explain exactly what you see happening, why it is bad, and how you feel about it. Focus on problem behaviors, not attitudes. Insist on corrective action. The Shirker is probably very practiced at giving excuses; be prepared to overcome them. "Two years ago, you carried a client load of sixteen, which was the office average. Since that time, the average caseload of your colleagues has risen to eighteen, while yours has fallen to twelve. Moreover, in the past nine months, four of the six complaints coming to my attention were ones that you and I had to resolve. I came in over the weekend to study our client files and found no evidence that your clients are any more demanding than others. Therefore, I have made reassignments that raise your caseload to fifteen, and I expect you to assume responsibility for the next three new clients we get." (3, 4)

✔ If the shirking is a recent phenomenon, talk with the employee to learn what may have caused the change. (2)

✔ Give the Shirker a greater sense of job ownership. Convey how much you count on her. "Let me explain why your job is so important to the future of the firm as well as to my current priorities. . . . Do you have ideas for how we can improve your results? What can we do to make your work even more personally satisfying?" (8)

✔ Be empathetic. Ask yourself, "If I were this Shirker, what would it take to get me to make the changes I am looking for?" Ask for suggestions from other trusted employees. Respond. (2, 6)

✔ If the behavior has been going on for some time, create a performance contract with the Shirker that clearly lists each of your expectations, quantifies successful performance, describes exactly how and when you will measure that performance, and states the consequences of failure. "I want a written plan from you with five new behaviors you will employ to serve these clients better. I'll approve that plan, and we'll incorporate it into your performance review. You and I will have reviews quarterly, instead of yearly, until we are both satisfied with the results. If this doesn't work, we can discuss the possibility of your finding a job outside the firm that's not as demanding."   (1, 3)

# The Sycophant

## *"Anything you say, Boss."*

- Praises you frequently and effusively.
- Is not likely to bring you bad news for fear of losing favor with you.
- Laughs at your jokes, even when they're not funny.
- Never offers an opinion without first asking for yours; then agrees with you. Never finds anything wrong with your ideas.
- Makes it clear to you that you are the country's smartest, most considerate, and most generous boss. (Sometimes you're not.)
- Doesn't rock the boat; always goes along with the program. Rarely expresses dissent in staff meetings.
- Can be malicious with peers—outdoing them for your favors. The most dangerous Sycophant is one who tries to look good by making others look bad.

## Avoid

✗ Believing what the Sycophant wants you to believe, i.e., that you are the best boss that ever was and that you walked on water to get there.

✗ Responding in kind by making the Sycophant a favored employee. Don't become a Pet Owner.

✗ Reinforcing the behavior of the Sycophant by showing a weakness for flattery.

✗ Overreacting to the Sycophant by becoming suspicious of every positive comment made by your employees.

## What to Say to Get What You Want

✔ Examine your behavior for things that you may do to encourage subordinates to behave as Sycophants. How do you mete out merit increases and other rewards? How do you behave during staff meetings and performance appraisals? If you don't want subordinates to flatter you, reward those who keep you out of trouble by *disagreeing* with you.   (2)

✔ Take a hard look at the relationship you maintain with *your* boss. Is there anything in it that employees might interpret as sycophancy and try to emulate?   (5)

✔ Make it clear that all news is good news. React as positively to information about problems as you do to information about successes. "That's not very happy news, but thanks for telling me. Now that I know the extent of the problem, we're in a better position to solve it—thanks to your honesty." (1)

✔ Tell the Sycophant that you do not appreciate his behavior. "I'm not sure where you got the impression that your job is to make me feel good, but please forget it. You'll make me a lot happier by being a top performer than by pumping up my ego. I never have thought much of boot-lickers, even when I'm wearing the boot." (3)

✔ Pull negative comments out of your subordinates. Encourage them to challenge your ideas. "Perhaps you've heard the saying that your enemy will make you laugh and your friend will make you cry. This idea needs a few friends at this point. We've devoted enough energy to documenting its advantages, so let's look at the potential downside. What might go wrong? Where are its weaknesses? Why *shouldn't* we implement it?" (4)

✔ When you conduct meetings and you want to make sure you get all ideas out in the open, appoint a devil's advocate. Ask for dissenting views. Tell people that you want your assumptions challenged. "Your job is to keep me out of trouble by preventing me from making foolish mistakes. I want each of you to take a few minutes right now to write down five potential disadvantages of my plan. Only when each of you is done will we proceed." (1, 2)

# The Short Fuse

*"You £#$%&*!+ |
&%#@$!"*

- Flies off the handle at the slightest provocation.

- Makes people reluctant to deal with or even be around her, because they don't know what will set off the next explosion.

- Short Fuses may have a powerful negative impact on employee morale and productivity.

- Behaves unprofessionally with coworkers, customers, employees, even superiors. Typical Short Fuse behavior includes shouting, name-calling, profanity, finger pointing, accusation, and foot-stamping.

- Is often a judgmental person who easily finds things wrong with others, an impatient person who must have her way, or an unhappy person who may be acting out personal frustrations. Sometimes the Short Fuse is merely modeling behavior she grew up with.

## Avoid

✘ Arguing; Short Fuses are already at such a high emotional state that they must calm down before they'll hear anything that you have to say.

✘ Walking away; if you don't stick it out, you can't modify the Short Fuse's behavior.

✘ Rising to the same level of emotionality, e.g., shouting, "Calm down!" Instead, bring the Short Fuse down to your emotional pitch.

✘ Accepting post-blowup apologies. Instead, press for a commitment that the behavior will end.

## What to Say to Get What You Want

✔ Examine your own behavior on two levels. Are you a Short Fuse yourself, and therefore a poor role model? Are you doing anything to light the fuse?   (5)

✔ Let the Short Fuse blow off steam, unless doing so will embarrass you or your customers. This cuts through the anger and calms the Short Fuse down, especially if you listen carefully.   (2)

✔ Respond slowly to the points made by Short Fuses. It will cut down the rate of explosion, and will enable her to hear the unreasonableness of her tone and words.

"Let..me..respond..to..your..concerns.
First..I..would..like..to..summarize..what..I..
heard..you..say. Listen..closely..to..
make..sure..I..represent..your..position..
fairly." (4)

✔ Speak calmly yet assertively when it is your turn in order to prevent the Short Fuse from exploding again. "Now just a minute, I would like to say something. Please hear me out with the same courtesy that I have just shown you. You'll have every opportunity to respond." (1, 3)

✔ Address the concerns of the Short Fuse specifically and directly. "What were the exact words that caused you to feel that way? Tell me how this situation prevented you from being able to do your job well. Give me all the specifics you can recall." (3, 8)

✔ Give the Short Fuse specific behavioral feedback on the negative impact of such behavior. "When you react that way, other people, including me, don't want to be around you. We're afraid to be honest with you for fear that you'll erupt." (3, 4)

✔ Stress the importance of professionalism, especially around customers. Insist that people on your payroll *always* act as adults, no matter what the provocation. Tell the Short Fuse to reserve tantrums for after working hours. "When one of your colleagues asked to see a copy of the report you submitted to me last week, you raised your voice and accused her of not trusting you. That unfortunate behavior occurred in front of three customers, who saw their first example of unprofessional behavior in this office. It will also be the *last* they ever see. You may lose your temper again, but it must never again be on company time." (3, 8)

✔ Get the Short Fuse to agree to end the behavior. "Yes, I heard you say you're sorry. But I'm waiting for something far more important than an apology: a commitment from you that this will never happen again." (3, 4)

# The Insubordinate

## *"That's* your *opinion."*

- Challenges your authority. May do so publicly, causing you to lose face in front of your superiors, peers, or other employees.
- Speaks disrespectfully to you, either in public or in private.
- Predictably challenges your requests; continually insists upon a rationale for what you are asking. What Insubordinates do isn't as destructive as how they do it. Their tone, airs, and insinuations can be infuriating.
- Criticizes you in front of coworkers, bosses, subordinates, customers, and just about anyone else who will listen.
- Violates procedures and accepted ways of doing things. Sees rules as something to be broken. A less blatant, but more insidious, Insubordinate is one who takes advantage of a close relationship with you to get out of tough assignments or procrastinate.

## Avoid

✗ Turning the other cheek or putting your head in the sand. If unchecked, the Insubordinate may breed clones.

✗ Getting angry, engaging in name-calling, or doing anything that will give observers reason to brand you as unprofessional. Don't try to get even. Insubordinates are digging graves for themselves; don't fall into one.

✗ Complaining about the Insubordinate's behavior to your boss or to coworkers. It will be rightly seen as a sign of weakness.

✗ Modeling insubordination yourself by disregarding organizational policies or by openly criticizing *your* boss.

## What to Say to Get What You Want

✔ Count the number of Insubordinates you have. More than two percent? What are you, or the organization, doing wrong to breed insubordination?   (5)

✔ Make sure you really have a case of insubordination, and not just an exuberant employee whose competency and sharpness scares you. Have policy, procedure, and rules actually been violated, or are stupid dictums being questioned? Are you being treated disrespectfully, or are your bad ideas

simply getting the challenge they deserve?
Many outstanding and dedicated employees
are treated as Insubordinates by frightened
supervisors.   (2)

✔ Spend some time with the Insubordinate,
giving the person the opportunity to talk
about himself, about you, about your
relationship, and about how he views his
role. "How do you feel about your job, your
contribution to the company, and our
working relationship?"   (3, 6)

✔ Confront the behavior directly. Tell the
Insubordinate exactly what you see
happening, why you believe it to be a
problem, and how you feel about it. "When
my boss asked for current production data at
the staff meeting, you interrupted as I was
responding and indicated that you, not I, had
the correct information. Whether or not your
assertion was true, which it did not turn out
to be, the tone of your response made it very
clear that you did not respect me. I was
embarrassed. Two people came up to me
following the meeting to say they found your
interruption out of line. Such unprofessional
behavior cannot be tolerated in this
organization."   (1, 3)

✔ If appropriate, elicit the Insubordinate's
recommendations for how to change your
perceptions. "What will it take to prevent that
situation from ever happening again?" In

hardened cases, you'll have to dictate the resolution and secure a firm commitment to new behavior. "The next time you feel I am about to present erroneous data, discuss it with me *before* the meeting. If that's not possible, whisper corrections to me at the meeting or pass me a note. That will be easy to do because you are going to sit next to me from now on. That is the exact behavior I expect from you. Do you have any questions?"  (2, 4)

✔ Document each instance of unresolved insubordination. You will need a "paper trail" if you ever decide to discipline or to terminate the Insubordinate. Most managers wait too long before creating a dossier on Insubordinates.  (6)

✔ Enlist your boss's help to back you up if push comes to shove. "One of my employees is causing some performance problems. Specifically, this is what is happening. . . . This is what I've done without success to correct the problem. . . . Unless you have any insights or suggestions, I'm ready to take more drastic action. Will you support a decision to . . . ?"  (10)

# The Hot Dog

## *"You're lucky you can count on* me.*"*

- Asserts a big ego and a need to win. The Hot Dog often tramples coworkers—and perhaps you—on the way to victory, creating morale problems.

- Gains the highest possible visibility on projects regardless of merit. Seeks the greatest glory for herself. (See the Back Stabber.)

- Puts her own welfare above the welfare of the team and of the organization.

- Strategically discloses, withholds, and uses information to promote herself. Lets people know things only when the Hot Dog will benefit.

- Seeks political alliances and liaisons throughout the organization for personal advancement.

- Is far more concerned that people *see* the quality of her work than that her work *is* of quality.

- Places style and appearance above substance and results.

## Avoid

✗ Being a glory-grabber yourself. Don't model the very behavior you are trying to stop.

✗ Rewarding the Hot Dog's behavior, even in subtle ways. Don't let showing off pay off. For example, don't praise an employee who achieved excellent results at the cost of hurting the team.

✗ Expecting this problem to go away by itself, or waiting for someone else to solve it. The Hot Dog must be checked. One of the worst morale problems occurs when subordinates lose hard-earned credit to a Hot Dog.

## What to Say to Get What You Want

✔ Find out if you appear to have more Hot Dogs than your colleagues. If you do, your employees may see you as hogging so much of the glory that they're reacting to get their fair share. Be a team player yourself.   (2, 5)

✔ Give as many rewards as you can to the team as a whole. Emphasize these rewards above the rewards you give to individuals.   (8)

✔ Hire team players over "Lone Rangers," no matter how talented they may be.   (1, 5)

✔ Continually make your expectations for team behavior known throughout your staff. Put them into writing.   (1, 3)

✔ Discipline individuals who use information strategically for their own gain, or who succeed at the team's expense.   (3)

✔ In your performance reviews of employees, never compare one to another. Be certain to evaluate teamwork. Emphasize results over style, form, and appearance.   (5)

✔ Confront Hot Dogs directly and immediately. Point to specific incidents. "The boss just called to congratulate me, and especially to commend you, on the two big contracts we just landed. When I asked him why he thought you had played such a major role, he said that you had told him the business came from two of your accounts. What you didn't tell him was that neither of those contracts were from the same divisions you work with; nor did you point out that it took over nine months of intense effort from your colleague Jean to get that business. Everyone on our team made a contribution, but yours, like mine, was in a supportive role."   (3)

✔ Tell the Hot Dog why her behavior is inappropriate. "We are a team. When any of us seeks individual glory, the cohesiveness of the team is diminished and our productivity suffers."   (1, 3)

---

✔ Make the Hot Dog clean up her messes. "I want you to call the boss as soon as you get back to your desk to clear this up with him. Handle it any way you like, but fix it so Jean gets the congratulations." (4)

✔ Insist upon a commitment to change. "If you intend to remain a member of this team, you'll need to give me your personal commitment to teamwork and to never allowing such a situation to occur again. Do I have it?" (3, 4)

# The Can-Do

## *"No problem."*

- Makes promises that are rarely kept.

- Eagerly volunteers for jobs, but doesn't complete them; takes on impossible workloads. Wants to do more important tasks with higher responsibility, but seems to lack the ability to succeed.

- Agrees to or suggests impossible deadlines.

- Often fails to deliver. His procrastination may be due to perfectionism, a fear of failure, or even a fear of success.

- Postpones unpleasant tasks in favor of fun.

- Follows through only when constantly monitored.

- Spends more time on giving the appearance of progress than on actual progress.

- Blames bad luck or other people when confronted with his failure to deliver, or says, "I knew you'd want it done right."

## Avoid

✗ Accepting unrealistic commitments.

✗ Giving the Can-Do the opportunity to volunteer for work beyond his ability.

✗ Entrusting work to the Can-Do you know he can't accomplish.

✗ Expecting a Can-Do to come around without help. The Can-Do's unrealistic self-perception means he is not likely to learn what's truly possible on his own.

✗ Shunting everything around or avoiding the Can-Do. You'll pay someone for doing nothing, and add to the person's confusion.

## What to Say to Get What You Want:

✔ If you have too many Can-Dos working for you, the fault may be yours. Perhaps you are fooled by job candidates who exude enthusiasm but little else. Alternatively, you might breed Can-Dos by not making it clear that you expect tangible results.   (5)

✔ Reject promises you don't believe the Can-Do will keep. Don't just say you can't trust the person or engage in any form of personal put-down. Report his track record as though you were giving the six o'clock news. "Actually, I don't want you to promise it that quickly. The last two times you made such a pledge, you weren't able to deliver either in timing or in quality. I remember, specifically, that . . . Those unforeseen glitches prove my point. This time I want you to plan realistically, with Murphy's Law in mind." (3, 4)

✔ Define assignments in terms of particular goals, explicit expectations, and definite, no-slip deadlines. Build in specific accountability. "This spec sheet shows exactly what the product must look like. Let's schedule brief meetings to review progress one month and ten days prior to delivery. And if either of us are dissatisfied with the headway you've made at those two points, we'll either get you some help or reassign the project. These may seem like rigid controls, but they're needed to ensure that we don't have a repeat of the time overruns on the last two assignments. What do you need from me or anyone else to guarantee success this time?" (2, 4)

✔ When you give assignments, ask the Can-Do to identify all the potential roadblocks. Anticipate their impact together and put him on notice that you'll be watching. "Imagine that it's three weeks from now. I'm in my office expecting to see the final product on my desk. You're in your office, trying to figure out how to give me the bad news that the work is not complete. What are the likely reasons you'll give me? . . . I'll be watching for those problems along with you to head them off. How can we plan to overcome them right now?   (2, 4)

✔ Maintain as much control as you can over the action, perhaps through intermediaries. Keep the Can-Do under close supervision and accountability.   (4, 5)

✔ Confront procrastination when it occurs; bring all the issues relating to it out in the open. "We're at week six in your project, and yet we've only attained the objectives of week three. What has prevented you from progressing beyond that point? What will it take to make up for lost time and be completely caught up no later than week nine?"   (3, 4)

✔ Praise the Can-Do when tasks are accomplished and deadlines are met. "Thank you for your efforts at staying on schedule. You really extended yourself by coming into the office over the weekend. I appreciate that."   (9)

# The Defeatist

## *"What's the use?"*

- Lacks motivation or desire to succeed.
- Feels pessimistic about her future. May have reached a plateau in the field or in the company.
- May have been passed over for promotions, or otherwise feels unappreciated, unfairly treated, or deceived by upper management.
- May have been a top contributor at one time, but now goes through the motions, with little enthusiasm, spirit, or spark.
- May be burned out by stress.
- Takes a pessimistic view of most projects. Regardless of what is proposed, this person sees the downside rather than the upside. The Defeatist is a ball and chain, spreading pessimism to others.

### Avoid

✗ Waiting for the Defeatist to "snap out of it." It won't happen.

✗ Accepting the behavior as reasonable, given what the Defeatist has experienced (e.g., a demotion). You're not being fair to her or the organization.

✗ Pep talks and "go get 'em" speeches. They only work in locker rooms.

✗ Chalking off the Defeatist as a lost cause. You can't afford what her lethargy is costing you. And you probably have a better chance of rehabilitating a proven employee than hiring someone as good.

✗ Enabling the Defeatist by allowing assertions of gloom and doom to go unchallenged.

## What to Say to Get What You Want

✔ Look at the situation through that person's eyes. Do you agree with the Defeatist's perception of mistreatment, unfulfilled promises, or blocked opportunities? If you don't, tell her as persuasively and as honestly as you can. If you do see the same handwriting on the wall, rectify what past wrongs may be of your doing.   (2, 7)

✔ Ask a trusted colleague for a candid opinion of the role you may be playing in the problem, and any suggestions for how to turn the situation around.   (5)

✔ Look for ways to enrich the Defeatist's job. What can you do to restore challenge, recognition, accomplishment, importance, growth, creativity, independence, involvement, ownership, and excitement? Can you give the person a major new assignment with high visibility that she would see as a plum—perhaps the chair of a company-wide task force?   (7, 8)

✔ Examine your own behavior to make certain you're not modeling pessimism to your employees.   (5)

✔ Focus the Defeatist on the absolute worst thing that can happen. Often she will find that this outcome is not nearly as bad as what is already resulting from her negative attitude. Or the Defeatist may realize that the worst case is unlikely to occur. "When we meet tomorrow, I'd like you to come with a written description of the worst-case scenario, along with a probability statement of its occurrence, based on hard evidence, not mere speculation."   (6)

✔ Help the Defeatist see what in her personal life may be contributing to the problem. Recognize that you'll not be able to affect these factors. "Are there other pressures in your life right now, which may be none of my business, that are contributing to your pessimism?"   (6, 7)

✔ Engage the Defeatist in a coaching and counseling session, with plenty of opportunity for her to be candid about her feelings and about you. Offer whatever you can in exchange for the performance you must require. "Even before I appointed you as assistant head nurse last year, I recognized your great future in hospital administration. Unfortunately, the head nursing position opened up before your bachelor's program was complete. In accordance with hospital policy, we had to offer it to someone who already had a degree. I feel bad about that and, as I promised you then, you will be eligible for advancement as soon as you get that sheepskin. My concern right now is the decline in your performance since we hired the new head nurse. As I've just documented for you on the Performance Review Form, your work has changed from 'consistently *exceeds* job standards' to 'consistently *meets* job standards'—a rating that won't justify your promotion to management the next time a head nurse position opens up. Before we talk about strategies for improvement, why don't you tell me how *you* see the situation?"   (2, 8)

# The Drain

*"I promise this'll be the last time I ask you about this."*

- Demands more attention, discipline, and coaching than all your other employees combined.
- Seems to forget what you said to do, how to do it, or when the task is to be completed.
- Asks for the same information repeatedly.
- Creates problems for your other employees. They often have to pick up the Drain's slack and feel he robs them of their time with you.
- Saps your energy and patience.
- Is capable of performing well, but at a prohibitive cost (measured by your time and energy).

### Avoid

✗ Blowing up at the Drain. Emotional outbursts simply label you as an irrational boss, incapable of solving a personnel challenge. Don't exacerbate your problems.

✘ Allowing the Drain's coworkers to use his behavior as an excuse for poor performance on their part.

✘ Enabling the behavior to continue. Don't make it easy for the Drain to sap your attention.

✘ Bad-mouthing the Drain to his coworkers. Employees believe that if you talk pejoratively about one of their peers behind his back, you'll also talk about them behind their backs. They're probably right.

✘ Waiting for the next scheduled performance appraisal before saying anything to the Drain. Waiting simply makes the situation worse. The appraisal session will be frustrating for both you and your employee.

## What to Say to Get What You Want

✔ Look around. How many Drains report to you? If most of your employees seem to be Drains, the problem rests with you and upper management, not with them. If employees don't receive goals, direction, resources, and training, they're absolutely justified in seeking your guidance and counsel.   (2, 5)

✔ When you delegate assignments or give directions, ask the Drain to repeat what you said in his own words. Don't be threatening.

"Just so I can be sure I told you everything I needed to, could you please tell me what you heard and what you think I expect." (3)

✔ If the Drain leaves out or mixes up information during this summary, tactfully correct him. "No, that's not exactly right. What I want you to do is . . ." (3, 4)

✔ After the Drain has correctly summarized your intentions, ask, "Do you have any questions about this job?" Answer them clearly. (2)

✔ Tell the Drain when his behavior is creating problems for you. Focus on the behavior, not the person's motives or personality. "When you seek me out three or four times a day, you take me away from other important duties. I'm happy to help you achieve your goals, but no employee should receive a disproportionate amount of time or energy from a boss. It's not fair to me, your coworkers, or you." (3, 6)

✔ Contract for improved performance. Specify what you want the Drain to do, how you'll help, and when you expect change to occur. "In order to correct the problem we're having, I'll provide you with the coaching we both think you should receive. After six weeks, if you aren't working more independently, the next course may be reassignment or dismissal. I know you can improve, and I want to help you." (3, 4)

# The Fountain

*"The project that you assigned to me last month has now arrived at the stage of development where I'm able to brief you, with great confidence, on the progress so far."*

- Doesn't get to the point; elaborates on unimportant or peripheral information before revealing her message.

- Rambles when making presentations or asking questions. The Fountain's briefings are never brief.

- Talks too much on the job; may socialize excessively.
- Tells you stories and information you've heard before—perhaps several times.
- Uses fifty-dollar words when five-dollar words will do fine. The Fountain can be a highly pretentious colloquist.
- May not listen well. A busy mouth leaves little time for ears to operate.

## Avoid

✗ Hoping the Fountain will shut off spontaneously. She costs you money by costing you time. The Fountain takes longer to do her job; distracts coworkers from their jobs; and fails to deliver the crisp, clear communication your schedule demands.

✗ Showing your displeasure indirectly. The Fountain will only be confused by your frustrated looks or avoidance. The Fountain is likely to attribute this behavior to a character flaw in you, or to become even more nervous (and talkative) when reporting to you.

✗ Assigning the Fountain jobs where her windiness will hurt other workers' productivity or give customers a poor impression.

✗ Telling the Fountain that she says too much. The Fountain will either get defensive or stop talking altogether. People who talk or write too much need specific feedback on why it's a problem and how to communicate effectively.

## What to Say to Get What You Want

✔ Verify that others see the Fountain in the same light, to ensure that no prejudices have affected your impression. For example, managers who feel threatened by the capabilities of the people who report to them sometimes believe they're faced with Fountains. Their employees may actually have a lot of important information to report.   (2)

✔ Search your own behavior for what you may be doing to turn on the Fountain. If you haven't made your expectations clear, she may be telling you everything she can think of, in the hope that something will hit the right button.   (5)

✔ Model the concise communication you expect from your employees. Give your department examples of the communication you want as well as what you'll reject.   (5)

✔ Assign Fountains to jobs where their excessive chattiness will be confronted and challenged by peers dedicated to work. A Fountain does less damage in some positions than in others.   (4)

✔ Point out the problems created for you. "When two people working side by side are involved in a conversation, they aren't concentrating as fully as they might on their work. Of course it's okay for people to chat when we're on break or have time to relax. But when anyone in this office is under the gun, socializing interferes with productivity." (3)

✔ Appeal to self-interest. "People don't want to read any more than they have to. Many clients will never get to the second page of this letter. Your message here is too important not to be read." (8)

✔ Work out a contract with the Fountain for improved performance. "The next time you prepare to brief me, imagine that you're a newspaper reporter whose editor will allot only seventy-five words for a front-page story. Start by giving me the headline." (3, 4)

# The Disappointment

## *"I'm trying as hard as I can."*

- Doesn't meet your expectations for performance. May do any one of the following: communicate poorly, not keep you informed, display inappropriate personal appearance, be frequently absent or late, squander time, be disorganized, be inefficient, waste resources, produce poor work, exercise poor judgment, or supervise ineffectively.

- Poor performance is usually attributable to one of these conditions: your performance standards are not known, you don't supervise well, you are a negative role model, training is inadequate, necessary resources are lacking, the employee feels underpaid or otherwise exploited, the employee lacks ability or desire, or the employee suffers from personal problems (e.g., addictions).

## Avoid

✘ Waiting for a miracle to happen. Act now.

✘ Focusing on the Disappointment's attitude; you only care about the person's *performance*. You can't change attitudes, you can change performance.

✘ Addressing the problem while you are angry.

## What to Say to Get What You Want

✔ Be certain your performance standards are known. Look into the adequacy of training, the provision of resources, and the recruitment and selection of employees. Honestly examine whether you are expecting too much given the pay and other tangible rewards provided. Get some feedback from others (e.g., your boss) on the negative contribution *you* may be making.   (1, 5)

✔ Talk with the Disappointment, asking questions to find out exactly what may be causing the poor performance. Focus on behavior at work. Do not pry inappropriately into personal affairs. "Over the past two months, I've noticed a decline in the quality of your work. Twice I've had to ask you to clean up your area; three valid complaints were received from your customers; and then there was that argument between you and your coworker. Is there anything I should

know about that's causing these problems?"
(3, 7)

✔ If you suspect that the problem is related to substance abuse or another matter with legal or criminal implications, consult with your human resource department or employee counseling/wellness center before proceeding. (2)

✔ Enlist the help of anyone else who you feel has a good perspective on the situation and understands the Disappointment. This may include your boss, your colleagues, or even coworkers of the employee who can help you confidentially. (2, 10)

✔ Given your knowledge of the Disappointment, ask yourself, "What's in it for this person to change? What appeal to self-interest might give me the results I need?" (8)

✔ Given your analysis of the situation, give the Disappointment direct, yet nonpunitive feedback. Contract for improved performance. "One of the standards of performance in our office is professional appearance. In the last few days I have noticed that your appearance is not what it used to be. For example, the clothes you're wearing today are wrinkled and have what look like food spots. The same was true yesterday. Your shoes have mud on them and are seldom polished. In this business we have to dress with regard to others' impressions. Your physical appearance says a great deal about this company, and that message must always be a positive one. Are there extenuating circumstances I should know about? If not, I'd like you to agree to do the following. . . . "   (3, 4)

✔ When the Disappointment makes measurable progress, acknowledge it. "Thanks for the effort you've put forth to sharpen your appearance. That shirt looks good on you."   (9)

# Coworker Advisories

*When a colleague is making your work difficult, remind yourself that your coworkers are not your responsibility. Many of the counterproductive behaviors described in these nine advisories should be addressed by superiors. Only if someone interferes with your ability to do your job well do you have a mandate to take action. Before applying these advisories, you may want to let the boss know what you are up to. You'll also want to consult with trusted colleagues.*

*Be prepared for the resentment that might be generated by your intervention into the behavior of a colleague. It might come from any of several sources, most likely from the person you're trying to help. Of our four groups of advisories, you are most likely to be accused of meddling when directing efforts at coworkers.*

# The Dead Weight

## *"Could you lend me a hand again this afternoon?"*

- Is primarily concerned about his own career.
- Doesn't carry a fair share of the load; gets away with as little as possible, transferring responsibilities to you and other coworkers. (See the Shirker.)
- Is unreliable; almost never delivers on promises to help or cooperate with you.
- Can't be counted on to pick up the slack when you're gone or to cover for you when you're under the gun.
- Is not a team player. When finished with his work, doesn't look around to see who else needs help. Actually makes more work for others who must compensate for the Dead Weight's incompleteness and errors.
- Creates a severe morale problem among those who work hard.

- Often complains about having too much to do, which is often the truth, because the Dead Weight hasn't been keeping on top of responsibilities. Accumulates a backlog of work, then may ask you to help "for the good of the office."
- Takes advantage of all sick days—especially on Mondays and Fridays.
- Turns lunch hours into sixty-five minutes—not quite enough to raise the boss's ire.
- Takes advantage of "official business" opportunities outside the office to get personal business done and to otherwise escape work.

## Avoid

✗ Tolerating the Dead Weight or taking on his work. You merely reinforce the behavior.

✗ Simply avoiding this coworker. The performance of the team is suffering. And even if you manage to stay out of his way, you'll continue to be upset by the Dead Weight's malingering.

✗ Talking about the Dead Weight behind his back to other coworkers. A few of them may support the Dead Weight but not tell you. When it comes out, the Dead Weight will feel further justification for not working hard.

✗ Confusing the Dead Weight by responding

negatively without stating your specific concerns.

## What to Say to Get What You Want

✔ Examine your personal prejudices. Could it be that your reaction to this coworker is somehow clouded by racism, sexism, regional bias, or religious intolerance? Consider whether most of the supposed Dead Weights you encounter are of the same gender, race, origin, or religion.   (2, 5)

✔ Ask trusted colleagues for their perception of this person, of your role, and what you might do. "I'm beginning to feel he takes advantage of me. Do you think I'm accurate in interpreting his absences, deadline failures, and requests for help as unnecessary burdens on our team? What would you suggest to turn this situation around?"   (2, 6)

✔ Meet with the Dead Weight. Play the role of reporter. Tell him what you see and why it's a problem. Don't attribute intent; talk instead about the consequences of the behavior for you, for your coworkers, and for him. Remain unemotional and controlled. "This afternoon the entire staff dropped what they were doing to meet the deadline crisis. We pitched in so that the office would come out smelling like a rose. However, as soon as the crisis was identified, you stayed behind that door and did your paperwork. The rest of us now have unfinished paperwork to take home this weekend. This is just one of the examples we've seen lately of selfish behavior. Can we come to any other conclusion except that you aren't carrying your share of the load?"   (1, 3)

✔ Provide incentives or encouragement, no matter how subtle, to change. For example, when the Dead Weight does assist you, go out of your way to acknowledge the help. Keep it brief. At the same time, don't let up on your negative reinforcement of any hurtful behavior; otherwise, you'll enable the Dead Weight to feel justified with his or her overall performance. "Thank you for taking that phone call for me."   (8, 9)

# The Rumor Monger

## *"Wait till you hear this."*

- Gossips about other people in the office.
- Is more likely to pass damaging information than positive information.
- Likes to bring you bad news—especially about the negative opinions others have of you. Does this under the guise of helping you.
- Loves to secure private information about other people. Uses that information to embarrass them.
- Is a one-person grapevine in the office. Is the first to know and pass on any and all information. Much of this "information" is distorted.
- Swears you to secrecy—along with twenty other people.

### Avoid

✗ Falling into the trap of passing on the poison the Rumor Monger pours into your cup.

✗ Initiating rumors yourself. Don't expect others to refrain from gossiping if you do exactly that.

✗ Listening to the Rumor Monger's tales without responding in a way that makes it clear you do not approve of such behavior.

✗ Talking about the Rumor Monger behind her back, or expecting others to keep the Rumor Monger out of the grapevine. She's an expert at finding out what people have said!

## What to Say to Get What You Want

✔ Avoid the Rumor Monger as much as your job permits.   (10)

✔ At every opportunity, correct any distortions and untruths you encounter in the grapevine. "That's simply not the case. I was there—let me tell you what was said."   (1, 3)

✔ Whenever the Rumor Monger's gossip is at your expense, tell her you don't appreciate it, and that you are personally offended. "You say you didn't start that rumor. I have no way of proving that you did, but we both know that you were a party to passing it on without telling me. I won't tolerate a circulation of lies about what goes on in my department. The next time you hear something negative about me or my department, I'd like you to tell me immediately, and I promise not to ask you to reveal your source. Let's agree to have that firm expectation of each other."   (1, 4)

✔ If you choose to speak with the Rumor Monger on behalf of your team, specify the consequences of her behavior for the morale and productivity of the group. "As a result of what was being said about them, my staff wasted half a day calling our customers to reassure them." (3)

✔ In a confrontation, the Rumor Monger is likely to become defensive and deny having said anything. Before you speak, verify your facts. Make sure you know exactly what was said, when it was said, how it was said, and to whom it was said. Make denial impossible. (2, 3)

✔ If there is more than one Rumor Monger in the office, you may need to ask upper management to set up an information clearinghouse to satisfy the need people have for information. (4)

# The Leech

## *"You're not busy, are you?"*

- Takes up a lot of your time on the telephone, in your office, or in other ways.
- May spend an hour of your day talking about personal problems, the boss, sports, clothes, or any of a dozen topics unrelated to your current priorities. Often comes by under false pretenses (your priorities) and switches to small talk for the final fifty-five minutes.
- May be an advice-seeker who rarely listens to your suggestions or whose need for advice exceeds your time or capability.
- Diminishes your efficiency by sapping your time and energy. The Leech robs the organization of a valuable resource—you.
- Is usually oblivious to signs that you want him to leave your office. You may look at your watch, tap your pencil on the desk, or receive an important phone call, but the Leech *will*

finish telling you about his daughter's graduation ceremony.

## Avoid

✗ Becoming so hardened to Leeches that you give the heave-ho to friends who have a genuine need for a listening ear.

✗ Making it easy for the Leech to hang on. Don't respond to excessive requests for advice; don't say you have a few minutes to listen when you are pressured by a deadline; don't contribute to conversations that go nowhere.

✗ Acquiescing because you feel sorry for the Leech. Consider the importance of your work! But the Leech does deserve sympathy—no one has ever been kind enough to tell the person how much he or she bugs people.

✗ Calling the person a Leech; that's cruel.

## What to Say to Get What You Want

✔ When you don't want anyone to come into your office, keep your office door closed or pile papers on your chairs and on the floor. Other strategies are to get less comfortable side chairs or to position your desk so that passersby cannot so easily get your visual attention.   (4)

✔ If the Leech knocks on your door and asks if you are busy, say yes. If the Leech starts,

"May I see you?" or, "Do you have a few minutes?" say, "Yes, at about 3:30 PM. I'm trying this new time management system— what may I jot down as our topic?"   (4)

✔ You might choose to confront the Leech directly on the consequences of his behavior for your relationship and for productivity— both yours and the Leech's. "As part of my efforts to be efficient, over the past two weeks I've been logging how I spend my time: I find that I spend more time with you than anyone else. When I contrast that with people who deserve most of my time, it's clear what needs to be done. I have some ideas of what you and I can do to maintain the flow of our work-related communication while cutting in half the actual time we take from each other."   (1, 3)

✔ If you want to maintain a social relationship with the Leech, say so, but explain that for the sake of his work and yours you need to confine interaction to scheduled breaks and after work. "I'd like to hear about that, but this report on my desk is due by the end of the day and I need every available moment to get it out. I enjoy our chats, but my deadlines do not. For the next several weeks, I'm really going to be under the gun with this new project. Why don't we use the lunch hour to catch up with each other until things quiet down?"   (3, 4)

# The Back Stabber

*"I'll put in a good word for you with the boss."*

- Takes credit for your accomplishments.

- Whispers sour nothings in the boss's ear about you. For example, when something goes wrong of unknown causes, the Back Stabber may implicate you by saying to the boss, "I'm sure [your name] did everything possible to keep it from happening."

- Says one thing to your face and does the opposite behind your back.

- Looks for ways to undermine your influence and credibility with employees and customers.

- Promotes her career at your expense. May take prized assignments away from you or sabotage your work.

- May spread ugly rumors about you. (See the Rumor Monger.)

## Avoid

✗ Engaging in counter-back-stabbing. This makes you look bad and gives the Back Stabber a reason to retaliate. In fact, it may be that the Back Stabber is already motivated by a perceived dark deed of yours.

✗ Complaining to coworkers. This is a dangerous accusation—especially if others don't agree with you, or if it turns out that you didn't have your facts straight. You may also appear to be whimpering.

✗ Doing nothing. An effective Back Stabber may discredit you in the eyes of your boss, causing no end of trouble.

## What to Say to Get What You Want

✔ Examine your own contribution to this situation. Are you misperceiving this person's behavior because of insecurity, bias, or a lack of all the facts? Is all your information reliable? Get as much validation as you can before you draw the line. (2, 5)

✔ If you know only one person described by the characteristics listed above, that person may indeed be a Back Stabber. If you know many people who fit the description, their behavior may be justified by something you are doing. For example, you may not deserve the credit you think you do. Alternatively, a plethora of Back Stabbers may be the result of a culture of fear established by top management.   (5)

✔ Before confronting the Back Stabber, gather your evidence carefully. Have as many documented examples on hand as you can possibly get. Confront the Back Stabber with facts, not with innuendo, hearsay, and supposition. "I have two things here in front of me. The first is a stack of 456 contact sheets that my telemarketing department compiled for the past three months. They show a 120% improvement in renewed subscriptions over that time. The comments of customers recorded on these sheets also document that it was the telemarketing approach I implemented last fall that accounted for most of the increase. Next to the stack is this week's corporate newsletter, in which you are quoted as attributing the increase to the newspaper ads your department designed—which 92% of the people we called said they never saw. The editor tells me you called her to initiate the story. Do you prefer to resolve this situation here or in the boss's office?"   (4, 8)

# The Troubled Friend

*"My outside life
is none of
this company's
business."*

- Shows declining performance due to problems in any or all of these areas: marriage, children, parents, health, legal problems, financial setbacks, or substance abuse. Problems may be manifested in decreasing quantity or quality of output or in deteriorating relationships.

- Doesn't admit that the outside trouble is affecting work. Believes the problem is no one's business—not recognizing that declining productivity is everyone's concern. Denial is the Troubled Friend's standard method of coping.

- Doesn't realize how much effect he is having on others, especially on friends who care. Few people are willing to confront the Troubled Friend.

## Avoid

✗ Closing your eyes and ears, hoping the problem will go away or take care of itself. It won't. And if you don't help, maybe no one else will.

✗ Enabling the problem behavior. For example, alcoholics often get attention only when they drink, which proves to be an encouragement to continue drinking.

✗ Covering for your friend's screwups. Again, you are rewarding his unwillingness to confront problems head on.

✗ Accepting responsibility for the causes of, or the solution to, your friend's problems. The Troubled Friend is the only person who can solve the problem. You can only provide the understanding, the encouragement, and the support he needs to change.

✗ Moralizing or passing judgment. There are many reasons why people get into trouble. Those reasons are never as clear-cut as they look from the outside. And remember, "There but for the grace of God go I."

## What to Say to Get What You Want

✔ If there is anything the Troubled Friend is doing that is potentially dangerous to self, to customers, or to anyone else, bring it to upper management's attention immediately. (3, 10)

✔ Address the *manifestation* of the problem— the behavior at work. Help the Troubled Friend to see the consequences of the behavior. You may be in the best position to do this. "Frankly, I agree with the evaluation the boss gave you. Nine months ago there wasn't anyone in this organization who could outproduce you, but your productivity began to decline after that. It showed itself to me in three ways. . . . " (3)

✔ Remember that you are a coworker. You are neither a professional counselor nor the Troubled Friend's boss. Personal problems are beyond your control. Your goal is to make sure that this person sits down with either your boss or a professional counselor as quickly as possible. "I know how you feel about doctors, but I think it's critical that you see someone immediately so you can understand what's going on. Knowing you as well as I do, I'm convinced that something is sapping your energy. Why not go to the Wellness Center for a screening, and get a referral from them for a specialist who can bring back the person who helped put this department on the map." (7, 8)

# The Poor Soul

## "Sometimes I think people are laughing at me."

- Seen by others as a pathetic figure because of appearance, hygiene problems, or some social inadequacy or learning disability.
- May not be fully aware of the low esteem in which she is held by employees, coworkers, superiors, or customers. Often the Poor Soul is aware of derision, but doesn't let on.
- Is the object of cruel practical jokes that too many people go along with. (See the Jabber.)
- Is well-meaning and good-natured but just doesn't seem to be on target.
- Believes she is doing better than is really the case, as regards both performance and relationships with other people.

### Avoid

✗ Laughing at or in any way participating in the jokes aimed at the Poor Soul.

✗ Opting for subtle advice, such as putting self-help books on the Poor Soul's desk. Notwithstanding the success of the mouthwash commercial on TV, most Poor Souls either won't get the hint or will just be embarrassed. If Poor Souls knew how to take a hint, they wouldn't get to be Poor Souls.

✗ Allowing your discomfort to prevent you from approaching the Poor Soul.

## What to Say to Get What You Want

✔ Recognize that the Poor Soul's unfortunate behavior is saying something about the company. Until she changes, this message will continue to be communicated to potential customers every day. For example, if the Poor Soul doesn't dress professionally, that says to some people that the company is not professional. (However, if a handicap is the Poor Soul's shortcoming, the reflection on the company will be *positive*.)   (1)

✔ Have the best interest of the Poor Soul at heart. No one else has up to this point.   (7)

✔ When you meet with the Poor Soul, focus on specific behavior that she can change. If something is beyond the Poor Soul's control, don't give feedback on it. For example, telling the person that she's too short is not helpful, but you can suggest strategies that will take the focus off height. "Let me tell you what people are responding to. . . . "   (3, 4)

✔ If the Poor Soul has a personal hygiene problem, such as body odor or bad breath, be very sensitive and offer concrete suggestions. "When people speak with each other face to face, they communicate in many ways. Our expressions, the gestures of our hands, even the odors of our bodies become the bases from which people draw profound conclusions about us. For example, bad breath can affect people negatively. Whatever the cause, people smell it when we talk and they react badly to us. Unfortunately, we often don't notice it ourselves. I count on my wife to tell me when my breath is offensive; today you can count on me. Let me make a suggestion that I think you may find helpful: you could visit a dentist for ideas. If you don't have one you like, I can make a recommendation."  (4, 7)

# The Empire Builder

## *"There's no question which department deserves the bulk of the allocation."*

- Cares far more about the welfare of his department than about the good of the organization.
- Maximizes outcomes within his department without concern for the effect on other departments.
- Cares more about what the organization can do for the Empire Builder than vice versa.
- Fights for maximum resources for his department without concern for what that leaves other departments or what it costs the organization.
- May claim credit for something your

department accomplished. (See the Back Stabber.)

- Develops proposals for upper management on ways to increase the department's size or his span of control.
- Welcomes increased responsibility that results in increased visibility and ultimately increased stature.

### Avoid

✗ Slugging it out toe-to-toe. The Empire Builder is probably more adept and devious than you are.

✗ Maneuvering behind the scenes. The Empire Builder will take that as a direct threat and work even harder to undermine you.

✗ Turning into an Empire Builder yourself. Your organization, and perhaps you, will end up the loser.

✗ Making imperialism easy by not fully asserting your own needs with your superiors.

✗ Using your employees as soldiers in a war against the Empire Builder's forces.

### What to Say to Get What You Want

✔ Give your boss rational, statistically-backed arguments for the resources you require. Emphasize potential benefits to the company, not your department. Put yourself in the boss's shoes and ask the question: "Why is it in my boss's best interest to treat me at least as well as the Empire Builder?"   (3, 8)

✔ Confront the Empire Builder, as appropriate. Be specific, clear, and demonstrate your unwillingness to be intimidated. "Our mandate is to balance the interests of our departments with the overall best interest of the company. In the meeting this morning when we and the boss were trying to allocate the excess $250,000, I found your argument to be out of balance. The other department heads feel the same, and have asked me to speak to you about it. For the sake of our ability to work together, and with the welfare of the company uppermost in our minds, let's look for a compromise that we can all live with."   (3, 4)

✔ Attempt to understand the Empire Builder and the root causes of his behavior. Search for a self-interest that might encourage the Empire Builder to behave in a more cooperative way. Fear is an effective motivator here. Can you get the Empire Builder to see a highly undesirable consequence of not cooperating? "The work of your department is too important to jeopardize in a battle against the rest of us."   (6, 8)

✔ As soon as you and the Empire Builder arrive at a point where you can no longer negotiate productively on your own, bring in your common boss as a mediator. However, in urging the boss to step in, don't complain about the Empire Builder. Make a case for the need to avoid conflict in the organization. "We pay a dear price in productivity when department heads fail to share the same goals." (8, 10)

# The Jabber

## *"I hope you won't take this personally."*

- Pokes at your sensitive spots, often under the guise of a good-natured ribbing or helpful advice.

- Reveals your vulnerabilities in front of others.

- Patronizes you. The Jabber may address you as a child.

- May jab even while expressing concern for you ("Are you worried about how your presentation will go?") or another person ("Don't fret; Debbie here has made that mistake many times").

- Can apologize quickly and easily. Unfortunately, the Jabber sees her apology as canceling out the insult, so she can jab you again.

- Engages in practical jokes.

- May criticize people behind their backs. (See the Back Stabber, Rumor Monger.)

## Avoid

✗ Doing nothing, or merely avoiding the Jabber. Someone's got to slow her down.

✗ Letting the Jabber upset you without also taking steps to stop the needling. She *wants* to get a rise out of you. Use your emotions to show the Jabber the serious consequences of such behavior.

✗ Answering the Jabber's patronizing questions exactly as she poses them. Take control of the conversation.

✗ Laughing at the Jabber's practical jokes, or letting them go unchallenged. Next time you may be the victim.

✗ Listening to the Jabber ridicule other people, especially behind their backs, without objecting. If she's doing it to them, she's doing it to you.

✗ Accepting the Jabber's apology without a commitment to change. A simple "sorry" won't be the end of the situation.

## What to Say to Get What You Want

✔ Seek confirmation from people you trust that they view the Jabber as you do. If not, examine yourself. Does your behavior attract repeated criticism? Do you have weak spots you're trying to hide from yourself? Are you sensitive to hearing the truth?   (2, 5)

✔ If the Jabber needles you on the basis of your sex, race, religion, or other personal qualities, that's discrimination. You're entitled to have it stopped. Tell your boss or personnel officer.   (1, 3)

✔ If you have a difficult challenge coming up, keep out of the Jabber's path as much as you can. Meanwhile, pump yourself up with positive self-talk. When the Jabber brings up the challenge, tell her what you told yourself. "Worried about that presentation? It's going to be a *marvelous* chance to sharpen my podium skills. I'm looking forward to it!"   (5, 6)

✔ If the Jabber approaches you with fabricated sympathy, surprise her by taking control of the discussion. When she asks, "Are you feeling all right today?" answer, "Why do you ask?" If the Jabber continues to profess interest in your well-being, say, "I feel just great! How are you today?"   (6)

✔ If the Jabber embarrasses you in front of other people, respond on the spot—she won't expect it. Furthermore, the others are likely to support you. "That's a very inappropriate comment to make in front of all of us." Expect to hear something like, "I'm sorry if I embarrassed you." Tell the Jabber, "You didn't embarrass me—I think you embarrassed yourself."   (4, 8)

✔ If the Jabber needles you on a sensitive spot, say, "Given the way you know I feel about that subject, I see your comments as hurtful." Again, the Jabber may answer that she didn't mean to hurt anyone. Don't back down: "Well, you did hurt me." End the discussion with, "You should think more about how your comments will make other people feel."   (3, 6)

✔ The Jabber will often say she's just kidding. Let her know you don't see such behavior as harmless. "Most psychologists agree that frequent kidding is a passive-aggressive way of attacking someone else."   (3, 6)

✔ Before accepting an apology, obtain a commitment that the Jabber won't repeat the behavior. "I believe your apology is sincere for you, but since you've done the same thing before, it's difficult for *me* to accept it. Instead, let's agree that you won't treat me that way again."   (4)

✔ When the Jabber denigrates someone who's not around, say, "I think that person has the right to hear your words first-hand." Let the Jabber wonder if you'll tell the person yourself.   (3, 4)

✔ In response to practical jokes, try a simple, "Not funny," a disgusted frown, and a swift, dignified exit.   (3, 10)

# The Know-It-All

## *"Let me tell you how to do that."*

- Offers information and advice at every opportunity, regardless of whether you asked for it, wanted it, or needed it.

- Speaks with a tone of certainty and authority, even when talking about something outside his expertise and responsibilities.

- Says or implies, "I told you so," if you suffer the least setback after failing to follow advice.

- Comes across as being in on all the important news and developments.

- Holds an inflated view of his importance to the company and the work group.

### Avoid

✗ Waiting for the Know-It-All to "get what's coming." Yes, the day may come when justice prevails. But there's no guarantee that just desserts will change the Know-It-All's behavior. And why wait for that day when your life is miserable now?

✘ Blowing up over the Know-It-All's smug, superior attitude. Your "immature emotions" will only reinforce the Know-It-All's sense of superiority.

✘ Turning down a good idea simply because the Know-It-All suggested it. Don't cut off your nose to spite your face.

✘ Sabotaging the Know-It-All's ideas and projects. Any attempt to do in a coworker will return to haunt you.

## What to Say to Get What You Want

✔ Ask yourself if you work with a lot of Know-It-Alls. If you do, you might be overly defensive when your coworkers coach and counsel you. If your performance has slipped and many people are offering you suggestions, you could be lucky enough to work with a group of concerned friends. (2)

✔ Tell the Know-It-All that advice has more impact when requested. "There's a natural reaction for professional people to become a little defensive when someone else tells them how to do their jobs." (3)

✔ Explain that advice is not destructive, but the tone in which it's communicated can be.

Focus on the Know-It-All's behavior rather than whatever you think is his intent. "This morning when you told me your views on the only way to complete my project, you communicated with a tone that sounded smug to me. Whether or not you intended it, that's the effect it had. As a result, I found myself tuning out your advice. I don't think that's what you had in mind." (4)

✔ When the Know-It-All communicates, "I told you so," respond in a controlled fashion, emphasizing that such a message is neither appreciated nor productive. Focus on the consequences of the Know-It-All's remarks. "When we fail to follow your advice and it turns out to be true, we don't need to be reminded of it. That remark makes me feel like a child and hurts our working relationship." (3, 4)

✔ Give fair credit when the Know-It-All is right. Acknowledge but don't rub it in when he's wrong. "While our new product didn't face all the problems you warned about, your advice on dealing with other departments was helpful, and I want to thank you." With enough reinforcement, the Know-It-All should feel secure enough not to blow his horn all the time. (8, 9)

# Customer Advisories

*The group we call customers extends beyond the people who order your products or walk into your store. It includes your clients, if you're a lawyer, consultant, or social worker; your students, if you're an educator; and patients, if you're a doctor or nurse. Sometimes you'll even find it's valuable to think of people from other parts of your own company as customers.*

*Customers are the people for whom your organization works, so it is very important to satisfy them without compromising yourself. Because encounters with customers are often brief and irregular, you must make the best of the available time by behaving flawlessly and resolving problems quickly. Once a customer thinks he or she has been slighted, you have fewer chances to make up for it over time than you do with bosses, employees, and coworkers.*

*Three advisories—the Destroyer, the Derelict Guardian, and the Loudmouth—are most often appli-*

*cable in retail stores, waiting rooms, and other public places. Indeed, this entire section could serve as a manual for retail personnel on the treatment of customers.*

*Whatever your situation, do not violate any of your organization's customer service rules in following these nine advisories. When one of our recommendations varies from your company policy or professional norms, adhere to the latter.*

# The VIP

## *"I need to be taken care of—now."*

- Feels a sense of entitlement; is determined to get her way.
- Skips ahead of other people in line, calls you out of meetings, and does whatever it takes to make sure her needs are met first.
- Calls just as you're leaving the office or walks into your store five minutes before closing time, expecting you to attend patiently to every need.
- Expects preferential treatment as a friend of the boss, a big buyer, or simply a powerful person.
- Asks you to provide extra services, to share privileged information, or to ignore missed deadlines.
- When you don't give in, threatens to go over your head, to take her business elsewhere, or to tell others not to patronize your organization.

## Avoid

✘ Responding to threats with counterthreats. You don't want an ugly scene, especially in front of other customers. Don't go head-to-head emotionally.

✘ Challenging the VIP's credentials, or telling the VIP that she is no better that anyone else.

✘ Allowing the VIP to get away with behavior that may alienate other customers.

✘ Simply providing everything the VIP wants. This exposes you and your organization to further demands.

✘ Justifying or defending your organization's policies; they are givens, not debatable points.

## What to Say to Get What You Want

✔ Examine the possibility that your organization's actions may cause customers to feel that they have to be pushy to receive good service. Provide excellent service for all.   (5)

✔ Establish a clear policy in your organization on how to treat VIPs. If certain customers are to receive preferential treatment, all employees must know how to identify and deal with them. "I know the people from Acme can be pushy, but they represent 40% of our billings. If you can't help Acme people immediately, transfer the call to me."   (1)

✔ Provide any special treatment privately so other customers won't feel slighted or demand the same attention.   (6, 7)

✔ Empathize with the VIP's needs even if you can't meet them. Make the VIP feel important even if you can't treat her that way. "You must need that shipment very badly, and as soon as I'm able, I intend to see that you get it."   (6)

✔ When the VIP skips ahead of other customers in a line, ignore her to deal with those who came first. If challenged state, "I am waiting on customers in the order of their arrival." Say nothing more.   (3)

✔ If the VIP interrupts while you're speaking with another person, turn and say with a smile, "Oh, hello. How nice to see you. I'll be able to help you in a minute. Thank you."   (4, 6)

✔ If the VIP threatens to go over your head, indicate how disappointed you are and provide the information needed to do so. Follow the guidelines your manager has given you on handling problems. "I'm truly sorry that you don't feel satisfied. Since our goal is to provide you with the very best customer service, my manager will be happy to speak to you. She's not in right now, but if you'd like to call back after 3:00 PM, she'll be available for you." Then it's up to your manager to balance service to this customer with the imperative of backing up an employee doing his or her job.   (6, 7)

✔ Be assertive with an angry VIP. Stand up for the needs to be met in the situation, not for your rights. Don't debate positions; deal with the goals to be accomplished. "I want to meet your needs as fully as possible without being unfair to other customers. Here's how we can do that. . . . "   (3, 6)

✔ Ask clarifying questions. The key to remaining rational is to move from the "what" to the "why"—from the positions each of you is taking to the reasons you're taking them. For example, the customer may say, "You're not doing your job!" Don't debate your job description. Instead, respond with, "I'm disappointed you feel that way. What have I done to give you that impression, and how might I correct it?" The VIP's response is likely to give you either a new option for meeting the person's needs or an opening to restate your organization's policy.   (2, 4)

# The Deceiver

## *"This isn't the price that was quoted to me this morning."*

- Exploits weaknesses in your policies or products for personal gain.
- May return merchandise to you that was not purchased at your store, or return damaged merchandise for a full refund.
- May lie about the value of a service you provided in order to get it at a reduced price.
- May lie about competitors' prices in order to get you to agree to a lower price. (See the Negotiator.)
- May actually switch the price tags on items, or claim that you previously made a lower offer for your services.
- May lie about what an employee had told him.
- May initially ask for less than he really wants, hoping to increase the order later for the

same price. Or the Deceiver may hint at a big order to get special prices.

## Avoid

✘ Accusing the Deceiver of lying or having devious intent.

✘ Insulting or embarrassing the Deceiver.

✘ Getting angry or making a scene in the presence of other customers.

✘ Granting considerations to the Deceiver that violate corporate policy or run counter to the best interests of the business.

✘ Letting the Deceiver get away with deception simply to avoid confrontation.

✘ Appearing to criticize or failing to back up employees who the Deceiver claims gave him misleading information.

## What to Say to Get What You Want

✔ Make absolutely certain the customer is lying and is not merely confused. Be sure you did not make an error in pricing the product or service. If you're not positive, give the customer the benefit of the doubt.  (2, 5)

✔ Follow company policy.  (1)

✔ Remain calm and deal with the issue to be resolved, not the person's exasperating attitude.  (2, 4)

---

✔ Back up and praise employees who tried to do the right thing—especially when your resolution with the customer appears to run counter to their actions. "That employee was acting properly within the framework of her instructions. Actually, I'm proud of how she handled herself. It was her instructions that need to be let go, not her."   (5, 6)

✔ Listen completely to the assertions being made by the Deceiver. Do not interrupt until he is finished. Check out the Deceiver's claim if you need to. "I wasn't aware of that. I will be happy to verify what the clerk told you in order to give you the best possible price consistent with it. Please give me just a few minutes."   (2, 3)

✔ Point out the reasons why you are not able to accept the situation as presented by the Deceiver. "I'm sorry, there must have been some misunderstanding. We don't have a clerk here right now who matches the description you gave. The manager assures me this is the price, and that there are no plans to discount it. May I ring it up for you?"   (3, 6)

# The Complainer

## *"I have never seen such incompetence in my entire life."*

- Is upset about an inferior product, lack of selection, poor service, high prices, or a shortcoming in your facility.
- Nitpicks at even the smallest flaws in your product, in your operation, or in you.
- Often attributes absurd personal inconveniences to the most minute of your failures (e.g., a ten-minute delay in a delivery that caused her husband to lose a full day's pay).
- May make a scene in a loud, belligerent, or angry voice.
- May complain as a smokescreen for some problem she is not willing to be honest about. Other times the complaint may be valid, yet blown far out of proportion by other negative

experiences the Complainer has recently undergone.

## Avoid

✗ Giving the Complainer good reason to complain by providing less than the very best service and products.

✗ Feeling defensive or personally attacked; your job is to deal with Complainers.

✗ Counterattacking the Complainer or showing excessive impatience.

✗ Forcing other employees to deal with the Complainer, and thus earning their resentment.

## What to Say to Get What You Want

✔ Recognize that a complaint, when valid, offers a chance to correct what should have been done well the first time. It represents one of the finest opportunities you'll ever have to earn a dedicated customer. Complaints are assets.   (2)

✔ When you know you can satisfy a disgruntled customer, offer your "make right" plan *immediately*. Don't make the customer wait, beg, or negotiate. "You should not have to put up with less than the best. Please allow me to make this right by . . . "   (3, 7)

✔ Kill chronic Complainers with kindness; defuse them with love. "You are a prized customer around here; please let me get to the bottom of what happened."   (6)

✔ If possible, relocate the Complainer to a less public section of the office or store. Try to get the Complainer to sit down.   (2)

✔ Give the Complainer a good listening to, without interruption, so the person can vent and run out of steam.   (2)

✔ When the Complainer has wound down, speak slowly in calm, measured, and empathetic tones. Don't allow the person to interrupt until you are finished. (You showed her the same courtesy.) "I'm sorry; I thought you were finished. . . . Now please let me explain the situation. And if you will let me speak without interruption as you did, we'll have this problem licked in a few minutes."   (3, 5)

✔ Ask pointed questions, as needed, to get to the root of the problem. "Please tell me exactly what makes you certain that you received useless advice from our counselor." Notice how it may be more helpful to ask a question without tacking a question mark on the end. Compare the previous statement with: "Exactly what makes you certain that you received useless information from our counselor?"   (2, 3)

✔ Lose the battle to win the war; agree more than you should in order to win important concessions. "Look, to keep your business we'll go one better than that. . . . "   (6, 8)

✔ Propose options to break deadlocks. Get the Complainer to respond. "We both seem to be sticking to our guns here. Which of your needs would not be met if . . . ?"   (6, 8)

✔ If none of your options are agreeable, and no other solutions are in sight, ask, "What would like me to do?" Do it or explain why you can't.   (4, 6)

✔ Be prepared to do something surprising to get the attention of a crazed Complainer when few of the above steps have had any impact. You may have to agree with the Complainer forcefully to get a word in: [Loudly] "You're right; we have *not* served you well!"   (5, 6)

# The Sponge

## *"I'm not going to make an impulsive decision."*

- Asks seemingly never-ending questions about your service or product. Takes a lot of your time.
- Calls you on the telephone unnecessarily.
- Requests documented product information that goes beyond the readily available data and may require extensive research.
- May demand information you cannot provide.
- May want reassurances you cannot make.
- Procrastinates in making a decision about your product or service. The Sponge likes it, but won't commit to buying it.
- Makes demands on your time that are generally understood to be appropriate only when ready to buy, but doesn't buy.
- May ask for free advice or for help with a purchase decision that will not benefit you in any way.

## Avoid

✗ Getting angry or visibly impatient with the Sponge.

✗ Ignoring or walking away from the Sponge.

✗ Delegating the Sponge to an unwary coworker or subordinate.

✗ Attributing devious motives to the requests. The Sponge's needy behavior probably reflects insecurity.

✗ Allowing your productivity to suffer from Sponges.

## What to Say to Get What You Want

✔ Examine your behavior honestly. If you have more than your fair share of Sponges, it may be that you have become impatient with valid requests for product information.  (2, 5)

✔ Routinely put yourself into your customers' shoes to anticipate their information needs. Ask yourself, "What would I want to know before buying this product?" Better yet, ask others that question.   (6, 8)

✔ Ask the Sponge to specify all his concerns so that you can provide the data for an informed purchase. "Please dictate every possible concern you have about owning one of these, and I'll write them down. I'll try to locate information for you in our brochures and perhaps even in unpublished reports that take a totally unbiased view. I want you to make a good decision, so that we won't have an unhappy customer." (2, 8)

✔ When you're too busy to respond, ask the Sponge to come back. Suggest a specific time. "It'll take me a while to get that information, but if you'll call back tomorrow afternoon after 3:00 PM, I'll give it to you over the phone." (3, 8)

✔ Inundate the Sponge with lots of printed information, even more than he asks for. When you can share manufacturer's brochures or spec sheets, Sponges will feel that they have the "insider" information they want. (4, 8)

# The Negotiator

## *"What's it* really *going to cost me?"*

- Wants you to sell your product or service for less than the going price.
- Asks, "How much better can you do on that?" or, "What do you really need to get for that?"
- Asks you to throw in additional items or services. "After we discuss the trust you're setting up for me, can you give us some free advice on incorporating my sole proprietorship?"
- Takes advantage of slight flaws to get a markdown. (Some Negotiators create the flaws themselves while you're not looking!)
- Brings an ad or an offer from a competitor expecting you to match the price—even though the ads are out-of-date or the offers are vague.

### Avoid

✗ Agreeing to do anything that violates company policy, industry standards, the law, or common sense.

✗ Making a deal with one customer that might compromise you with others.

✗ Criticizing the customer for attempting to negotiate with you. When complaining to others about poor treatment, the Negotiator won't say why you were caustic.

✗ Saying, "Take it or leave it." This will anger the customer and probably lose the sale.

## What to Say to Get What You Want

✔ Have a clear understanding of company policy and procedure for dealing with Negotiators. You may even wish to suggest to your boss that some negotiating room be put into certain products and services to boost sales. (1)

✔ When negotiating is okay, make sure salespeople know when to bring the boss into the negotiation process. (3)

✔ Restate exactly what the Negotiator has asked for. This establishes the opening position. In cases where you have no freedom to bargain, this can embarrass Negotiators and encourage them to back down. "You're asking me to give you two of these shirts absolutely free with that suit?" (2, 6)

✔ When you are unable to negotiate, say so—without anger, without accusation, without guilt, and with a reason why. "I want your business and I really wish I could do that. Unfortunately, company policy won't permit it because the prices on these shirts are fixed and we must account for every bit of merchandise through our computerized inventory system. Frankly, if I gave you something, I'd have to make it up out of my own pocket." (5, 6)

✔ Offer the Negotiator some other form of perceived value, if possible. "If you're concerned about whether the suit is worth its price, let me point out other features that you may have overlooked. And, confidentially, you ought to know that when we have our clearance sale next month this will be one of the few lines *not* marked down. If you see something else you like, and it is going on sale, I might be able to get permission from the manager to put it away for you now." (8)

# The Non-Compliant

## *"I don't see why I need to."*

- Fails to follow your instructions when filling out forms, submitting information, or asking for service.
- Doesn't fulfill promises; treats deadlines lightly.
- Ignores signs that constrain behavior ("No Smoking") or provide assistance ("Press Button for Help").
- May openly challenge your right to expect certain behavior from your customers.
- May refuse to comply with your requests for the information or behavior that you need to give the best service.

### Avoid

✗ Assuming that your organization's needs are obvious to anyone with common sense. If your customers knew all about your organization, they'd be running it.

✗ Asking the Non-Compliant for any more cooperation than you really need.

✗ Giving the Non-Compliant false or exaggerated reasons for your requests. Don't claim that the law requires something if it doesn't. Don't hide your organization's real reasons for its policies. If the truth comes out, the Non-Compliant will start to suspect all your other statements.

✗ Accusing the Non-Compliant of being uncooperative or of intentionally sabotaging your attempts to serve. Putting the person on the defensive is likely to make things worse.

✗ Allowing customers to see each other breaking the rules. Don't give them any excuse to ignore your needs. Don't make one feel that he is treated more strictly than another.

✗ Demanding information or behavior from the Non-Compliant. Taking a hard position will either encourage the customer to do the same or will generate resentment.

✗ Covering for the lack of cooperation without letting Non-Compliants know the serious consequences of their actions. You'll have to do that again in the future.

## What to Say to Get What You Want

✔ Ask yourself if your company makes excessive demands for customers to submit information, fill out forms, meet deadlines, or conform to behavior standards. Ask a selection of trusted customers and knowledgeable employees.   (2, 5)

✔ Communicate your expectations to customers clearly and early; the most common cause of customer non-compliance is ignorance. A store may post friendly yet assertive signs: "Please help us to serve you better by having your photo ID ready with your completed check when it's your turn to check out." A professional may give clients a list of mutual expectations for their relationship.   (1, 3)

✔ At every opportunity, model the behavior you expect of your customers. Let the Non-Compliant see that you don't ask any more than you give.   (5)

✔ Fully explain the need for the required information or behavior. "The state Department of Health requires this information before they'll reimburse us."   (6, 8)

✔ Make sure the Non-Compliant recognizes whatever direct benefits will result from complying with your requests. "I understand your impatience as we double-check signatures, but if your credit card is ever stolen, you won't have to worry if the thief tries to use it here."   (8)

✔ Give Non-Compliants specific yet sensitive feedback on the problems caused by their behavior. "Not having this form completed will add another 15 minutes to the time of every patient in our waiting room. Please help us next week by filling out the form in advance." (3, 4)

✔ Make deals whenever you can. "If you're willing to look up that information for us, I'll give you an appointment next week that won't make you late for work." (8)

# The Destroyer

## *"Look at this! Oops."*

- Leaves displays damaged or in disarray, and waiting areas a mess.
- Ignores signs that say, "Please do not touch."
- Handles objects with little care for their safety; spoils them, puts them down roughly, may even drop them.
- Unwraps packaged products; walks away, leaving them looking like secondhand merchandise.
- Leaves your establishment looking shoddy.
- Reduces the value of your inventory, equipment, or property.

### Avoid

- ✗ Looking the other way or crossing your fingers, hoping that nothing gets broken.
- ✗ Communicating hostile messages to all customers through poorly constructed,

negatively stated warnings throughout your store. Replace "You break it; you bought it" with "Please leave this display looking as nice as it does now."

✗ Hounding customers as though you don't trust them.

## What to Say to Get What You Want

✔ Keep an attractive store or office that looks too nice to spoil.   (1)

✔ Place fragile, easily damaged products out of the reach of customers.   (3)

✔ Make use of a limited number of attractively drawn, positively stated requests for cooperation from your customers. "Please enjoy your refreshments and tobacco products before coming in."   (3)

✔ Treat your customers very well. Kill Destroyers with kindness.

✔ Keep an eye on the Destroyer without hovering.   (6)

✔ If a customer is having trouble repackaging an article, do it yourself. "Please allow me to rewrap that for you—I've finally figured how it goes."   (5, 6)

✔ Confront the Destroyer directly whenever he is in the act of damaging a product; ask the person to refrain. "That is a very delicate product. Please let me help you get a better look at it by holding it for you. That will assure that if it is inadvertently broken, it won't be charged to your account, as store policy requires."   (4, 8)

✔ Ask habitual Destroyers to leave your store. "Unless you've come to pay for the damage done to our china display last week, I must ask you to leave." Call security if necessary.   (10)

# The Derelict Guardian

## "Children—what can you do with them?"

- Brings misbehaving children into your establishment. They may be screaming or crying, disturbing customers in some way, or damaging store property.
- Makes no attempt to control the children's problematic behavior.
- Is likely to be defensive about the rights of the children.

### Avoid

✗ Asking for trouble by making stock accessible to children. Put fragile items out of their reach.

✗ Reprimanding the children yourself. You will only upset the guardian, especially if that person is their parent.

✗ Wasting your time continually looking around the corner to keep an eye on those children or walking around picking up after them.

✗ Getting angry or losing your composure either with the guardian or the children.

✗ Judging the parent you are observing.

✗ Overreacting to children who may be loud or exuberant, but are not upsetting other customers or doing damage to your store.

## What to Say to Get What You Want

✔ Consider leaving out stock that children can play with—stock that you don't plan to keep in sellable condition.   (10)

✔ Inform the guardian about the impact of the children's behavior. Ask for the guardian's cooperation. "May I ask for your help in encouraging the [don't say *your*] children not to play tag in the aisles? It does seem to be disturbing the other customers in the store. I know how restless they can be on a shopping trip, and I really appreciate whatever help you can give us. Thank you."   (3, 4)

✔ Be more assertive (politely and firmly) if your request fails to get results. "I'm sorry, but we don't seem to be making any progress with the problem I brought to your attention a few minutes ago. Please remove the children from the store." Remember, if you do this, the customer may either be embarrassed and comply or may be offended and will criticize you for a long time to anyone who'll listen.   (6, 7)

# The Loudmouth

## *"IS IT POSSIBLE TO GET ANY HELP AROUND HERE?"*

- Is loud, rude, or profane enough to bother your other customers and your staff.
- Complains about your service in front of other customers as a way of intimidating you. A Loudmouth may voice complaints in a jocular tone—but will everybody get the joke?
- May make insulting comments about someone's sex, race, or appearance.
- May use profanity or slurs just loud enough to hear.
- May argue with other customers over a place in line, the last available item, or some issue totally irrelevant to your business.
- May even start a pushing match or fistfight.
- May offend in non-verbal ways, through dress or body odor.

- Often travels in packs. Loudmouths feel more secure together. Or two people may start to quarrel about a private matter, turning themselves into Loudmouths.

## Avoid

✗ Shouting back. Definitely don't shout, "Shut up!"

✗ Cowering before a Loudmouth, who will be emboldened by your retreat. You owe it to your other customers, your employees, and yourself to stop the offensive behavior.

✗ Accusing people of being Loudmouths. This will only give them another reason to be hostile.

✗ Taking sides in arguments or getting in the middle of them, either emotionally or physically.

✗ Taking any unnecessary risks. The Loudmouth in front of you may be easily provoked to violence.

✗ Discriminating against certain types of people. Not all groups of teenagers behave like Loudmouths, for instance.

## What to Say to Get What You Want

✔ Find out what your customers are saying about you. Conduct a survey or hold interviews to learn if they feel well served. If you don't anticipate and respond to their needs, you may breed a generation of Loudmouths who feel they must be aggressive to receive the service they want.

✔ Some managers prefer to have a boisterous place of business. Recognize two drawbacks: catering to loud people may encourage more offensive Loudmouth behaviors, and it may drive away customers who prefer a quieter atmosphere.

✔ Consider and plan for the disruptions likely in your particular organization. Don't get caught by surprise.

✔ When a customer speaks to you in an inappropriately loud voice, quiet that person by responding deliberately and softly. You may first have to get the Loudmouth's attention by being loud yourself, but don't stay at that level. "I understand you, sir! Now let me help you. . . . "   (5, 6)

✔ When the Loudmouth has a complaint, move the conversation away from the other customers. Then follow the steps for the Complainer, page 282.

✔ If the Loudmouth uses profanity or other offensive language, reply, "Excuse me. I can understand the importance of what you're saying, and I hope you equally understand our need to avoid the language I just heard." In order to be clear, you may need to restate the offensive words.   (1, 3)

---

✔ If the Loudmouth's clothes are inappropriate, this might work as an opening statement: "I'd like to suggest something that may help you feel more comfortable in our building." You may need to be more directive, but whatever you say must be consistent with your company's written guidelines. This is a delicate issue.   (5)

✔ If two customers are fighting over a store article or a place in line, approach them swiftly. Ask questions, listen, and mediate. "Let me see what I can do to help. I'd like you each to please tell me what's happening here without interruption. [Turn to one.] Would you please go first? [Turn to the other.] Then I will hear from you."   (2, 3)

✔ After getting the stories, suggest a solution. "In fact, we have another of those items in our window display. Let me get it for you." If there's no easy answer, make a small sacrifice to resolve the situation, "Is either of you willing to relinquish your claim on this item now in exchange for a 10% discount on the next one we have in stock?"   (8)

✔ Thank both customers for their cooperation. Reassure any customer who appears to have "lost" a dispute. "If you'd like, we'll make a later appointment for you right now."   (7)

✔ If Loudmouths are involved in a personal argument, politely and firmly tell them,

"Please move outside our office to complete your discussion away from our other customers. Thank you."   (1, 3)

✔ If two Loudmouths are fighting, firmly ask them to stop and leave. If they don't, call security guards or police.   (10)

# Action Plan

*Use these sheets to prepare yourself for dealing with difficult people.*

**Step One:   When you're faced with a difficult person, list his or her three behaviors that hurt your own performance the most.** Remember to concentrate on behaviors, not on what you see as the intentions behind them. Also, unless you can connect the person's behavior to a problem that you have a responsibility to correct, you'll have a hard time justifying corrective action.

1. _____

2. _____

3. _____

**Step Two:   Using the Index of Behaviors, classify this person as one or more of the types.** List as many as you think apply, starting with the most critical. Then reread all the relevant advisories for ideas.

1. _____

**2.** _____

**3.** _____

**Step Three:** **Indicate how well you believe you apply the Ten Commandments of Change when dealing with this person.**

*Fully*    *Partly*    *Not at All*

| Fully | Partly | Not at All | |
|---|---|---|---|
| ___ | ___ | ___ | 1. Expect the Best |
| ___ | ___ | ___ | 2. Listen Before Talking; Think Before Acting |
| ___ | ___ | ___ | 3. Get to the Point |
| ___ | ___ | ___ | 4. Change What They Do, Not Who They Are |
| ___ | ___ | ___ | 5. Model the Behavior You Desire |
| ___ | ___ | ___ | 6. Adapt Your Approach to the Person |
| ___ | ___ | ___ | 7. Provide for Dignity and Self-Respect |
| ___ | ___ | ___ | 8. Appeal to Self-Interest |
| ___ | ___ | ___ | 9. Rejoice at Success |
| ___ | ___ | ___ | 10. Cut Your Losses with Remorse, Not Guilt |

**Step Four:** **Based on your self-evaluation in Step Three, commit yourself to new strategies to deal with this person's behavior.** Start by reviewing the Commandments that you practice "Not at All": Are you missing opportunities? Then look at the Commandments you're "Partly" following: Where do you see opportunities to gain? Specifically, commit yourself to avoiding three ineffective actions you've tried or contemplated in the past:

1. _____
2. _____
3. _____

Commit yourself to three new responses. Decide what you'll say to get what you want:

1. _____
2. _____
3. _____

**Step Five: Do it!**

# Index of Behaviors

**In this book**, we've assigned types of difficult people to the categories where they appear most frequently. Some of the people you encounter won't be in those categories, however, or may combine the characteristics of two different types. So that you can easily find the best advice for responding to them, we've created this index listing the most common behaviors of each of the 44 types of people we've discussed. Skim through the list, noting which statements or primary behaviors are characteristic of the person you face. Then look up those advisories in Part II for the help you need.

# Index of Behaviors

# The
# *What to Say to Get*
# *What You Want*
# Seminar

## By Sam Deep and Lyle Sussman

This seminar builds on the knowledge you've gained from this book. It helps you to handle challenging people and achieve more of your goals, while keeping your relations as mutually satisfying as possible.

The focus throughout is on prevention, rather than resolution, because it is easier to head off frustrating situations than it is to react to them successfully. So this is less a seminar on dealing with irritating people than it is on keeping things from getting to that stage.

The Seminar will help you generate a plan for getting better results with a person at work who is troubling you right now. That person may be a boss, employee, coworker, or customer who goes against your grain by being too aggressive or too passive; by being too demanding or not demanding enough; by saying too much or too little; or by disappointing you in other ways.

**What will this seminar do for me?**

Here's what you'll come away with:

■ A positive identification of with which of the 44 cantankerous characters described in this book you need more success;

- Confirmation of just how common or unusual the tough people are that you encounter;

- Personal insights from the authors on how to practice the **"Ten Commandments of Change"** with difficult people;

- A test score that tells you how well you've been doing on each Commandment with the most frustrating person in your life;

- Recognition of why your current behavior with this person may not be the best;

- And, finally, a written plan for getting better results.

## How is it organized?

This seminar uses eight steps to help you deal more effectively with the challenging people in your life.

### Step One: Recognize your usual style with problem people.

Are you a hothead, sheep, magician, or problem solver?

### Step Two: Find the person who challenges you the most.

Is is someone you work for or with? Someone who works for you? Or someone you serve?

### Step Three: Take the "Ten Commandments of Change" test.

We created a 20-item test of your behavior with difficult people, based on the principles of this book. You'll take it with regard to the person you identified in Step Two.

### Step Four: Analyze your test results.

Are you happy with your grade on the test?

**Step Five: Congratulate yourself!**
You deserve credit for what you're doing well. We'll celebrate your success.

**Step Six: Acknowledge your violations of the commandments.**
What's preventing you from doing and saying all the right things covered in this book?

**Step Seven: Commit yourself to a new approach.**
What's your specific plan to become a better agent for change? What are you going to avoid? What are you going to do and say differently after this seminar?

**Step Eight: Get feedback on your approach.**
Seek advice from someone whose judgment you trust before executing your plan.

## Who should attend?

This seminar is for anyone who wants to get better results with challenging people. Who specifically will profit? **Sellers** who need greater rapport with customers; **secretaries** who want to please bosses and handle peers more effectively; **supervisors** looking to get more out of employees; **teachers** seeking better results with students, administrators, and colleagues; **health care professionals** who must deal with tough people in the health care milieu; and any **manager** (or **parent!**) who isn't happy about his or her success with others.

## What's special about this seminar?

1. Participants receive a signed copy of ***What to Say to Get What You Want*** and a comprehensive manual that provides all the information needed to follow the seminar leader.

2. Participants get **The Concentrator**—a unique tool that aids in understanding difficult people.

3. The seminar length is suited to your group— either a half day (3 1/2 hours) or whole day (5 hours).

4. Following the seminar, we can arrange brief coaching and counseling sessions for managers who will benefit from personal consultation.

5. The seminar design ensures that the insights participants gain apply to the difficult people **they** encounter. The book, the manual, and the instructor ensure that this seminar is tailor-made for each person enrolled.

6. **What to Say to Get What You Want** seminars are taught personally by either Sam Deep or Lyle Sussman, the authors of this book.

### Is this seminar available to my company?

**What to Say to Get What You Want** can be presented to your employees at the location of your choice. The ideal number of participants to invite varies; the typical audience size is in the 20–50 range. Following consultation with you, this on-site seminar is adapted to the environment within your company and to the development needs of your employees. To schedule the seminar or to receive a sample copy of the seminar manual, write or call:

**Sam Deep**
**Seminars by Sam Deep**
**1920 Woodside Road**
**Glenshaw, Pennsylvania 15116**
**1-800-526-5869**